OUR HERITAGE HAGGADAH

OUR HERITAGE HAGGADAH

*A Passover Celebration for Congregations and Families Seeking a
Deeper Understanding of Their Biblical Jewish Roots*

HEIDI EFROS-AFFRIME

ILLUMIFY MEDIA GLOBAL
Littleton, Colorado

OUR HERITAGE HAGGADAH

The views and opinions expressed in this book are those of the author and do not necessarily reflect the official policy or position of Illumify Media Global.

Published by
Illumify Media Global
www.IllumifyMedia.com
"Write. Publish. Market. *SELL!*"

Library of Congress Control Number: 2020903886

Paperback ISBN: 978-1-949021-96-7
eBook ISBN: 978-1-949021-97-4

Typeset by Art Innovations (http://artinnovations.in/)
Cover design by Debbie Lewis

Printed in the United States of America

CONTENTS

ACKNOWLEDGMENTS

I would not have felt qualified to publish this work if it weren't for the excellent training I received at Dallas Theological Seminary (DTS). A special thanks goes to my teacher and spiritual dad, Dr. Toussaint, who endorsed an earlier version of this work before his home-going in 2017.

I also want to thank my Hope of Israel family for encouraging me to publish this work: Kearicia and Barbara for assuming some of my responsibilities; Larry for encouraging me to introduce God's Personal Name; Pinky for your time editing; and Jim for your many historical insights and suggestions that always inspire my thoughts.

I especially want to thank my children: Lonnie, Julian, Faith, and Yin Tong, and my husband of thirty-nine years, Scott, for encouraging and empowering me in this endeavor. You offered your time in formatting and review, edits and suggestions, as well as scrutinizing the Hebrew. You also helped me to adapt this work to be more "user-friendly" for the Church at large, which may not be familiar with the Passover Seder. I especially want to thank Scott for being my spiritual leader and soulmate. We really do complement each other to be better than we could be on our own. Your believing in my creative abilities and urging me to reach a broader audience has led me on this journey to start publishing my work.

Above all, I thank my Heavenly Abba, Messiah Yeshua, and the *Ruach Ha Kodesh* (Holy Spirit) for giving me an insatiable desire to dig into Your Word to gain wisdom and understanding.

INTRODUCTION

I grew up in a reformed Jewish household. Every year we participated in large Seders that included 100–125 extended family members and lasted four to five hours.

It was a favorite event for me, as I got to see all my cousins and learn more about God's love for my people. I would imagine myself in the story and always had more questions than my family could answer.

When I was thirty, a professed atheist member of my family became interested in his Judaism. He ended up going to Israel to study and eventually became a rabbi. He challenged me to read my Tanakh (Hebrew Scriptures), seek a deeper understanding of Judaism, and live a more Jewish life.

I took his advice, and for the first time began to read the Bible my synagogue had given to me when I was confirmed at fourteen, an honor given to those children who go beyond Bar or Bat Mitzvah study to learn about their Jewish history.

As I read, I was perplexed to find that our Holy Scriptures revealed nothing that even hinted of modern Jewish Orthodoxy or any other branch of Judaism. I was also fascinated, and a desire to know more about God was rekindled in my spirit.

The more I learned, the more I felt embraced by God's unconditional love for my people even though we were so rebellious. What an awesome Father!

After reading the entire Tanakh in less than a year, I faced a new dilemma: I knew that the Torah spoke of God sending a "Moses-like Prophet" (even greater), and we were to be looking for him—but now I came across a plethora of Messianic prophesies I had never been told about (although they were familiar statements I'd seen on Christmas cards and heard in Christmas carols).

Eventually I couldn't ignore the fact that our history seemed to be interwoven with "His-Story."

Why didn't our rabbis or parents ever talk about this? Were my Jewish Holy Scriptures, given to me by my synagogue, actually telling me a Savior had come?

I realized I had grown up celebrating all the Jewish holidays based on the rabbinic traditions, not the ordinances of Scripture. My interest in learning more about God's Appointed Feasts was a result of celebrating my first family Seder as a Messianic believer. I finally had answers to my own childhood questions as I realized these Appointed Seasons of YHVH were foreshadowing "His-Story"!

I began going to a Christian church expecting I would surely gain a better understanding of these things.

Instead, I discovered that today's churches had completely removed these celebrations. I was disappointed and bewildered, but not shaken. I continued my quest to search out these mysteries on my own.

Yeshua told the Samaritan woman: *"But an hour is coming, and now is, when the true worshipers will worship the Father in spirit and truth; for such people the Father seeks to be His worshipers"* (John 4:23). To me, that verse has meant integrating my Jewish heritage and all of Scripture into my worship. That verse has only fueled my desire to "know Him and make Him known."

The result of that desire to know Him and make Him known is the book you now hold in your hands.

My prayer is that this guide to celebrating the Passover Feast in your congregation or home will feed your mind as well as your body.

If you are skeptical or simply unfamiliar with Scripture, I urge you to read the Bible for yourself and find out who God says He is—and in doing so, learn about His love and concern for you in a powerful and personal way.

It just might bless your life as it did mine.

1 PREPARING FOR THE PASSOVER SEDER

1

PREPARING

This Haggadah is a written guide that will walk you through the narrative and traditions of the Passover Seder, which means "order."

The word Haggadah means "the telling" and comes from the biblical mandate in Exodus 13:8: "And thou shalt tell thy son..."

The commandment to commemorate the Israelites' exodus from Egypt with an annual Passover feast was given in Exodus 12. That means the Exodus story has been recounted for about 3,500 years! Indeed, the last supper Jesus shared with his disciples was the Passover Seder.

We believe there is merit in participating in the Passover Seder, not only for the Messianic community, but for the Church at large. When we remember and share this story, we celebrate God's faithfulness in redeeming His Covenant people in fulfillment of His promise to Abraham. The Messiah Himself proclaimed this feast to be a foreshadowing of God's faithfulness in sending Him as "the Lamb of God, that taketh away the sin of the world" (John 1:29).

This book will offer directions and explanations to help churches (as well as family households that have never celebrated the Last Supper in a biblical way) enjoy a deeper experience observing the Seder that Messiah shared with His disciples.

This Haggadah also includes Jewish traditions that have been passed down over the centuries to assure that this historic event will be remembered throughout our generations. It is meant to engage both children and adults in a meaningful evening that they will want to relive from year to year. Traditional sections will be delineated in a manner that allows Seder leaders to include or skip over. (Skipping over portions of the Seder is not uncommon, even in most Jewish households.)

Reliving this story connects the Jewish people of today with the promises made to their ancestors (some still unfulfilled) and connects New Covenant believers with the full story of God's great love for all of us.

Following are the checklists and instructions you will need to prepare to host a Passover Seder for your congregation, community, or family.

2

ROLES TO BE ASSIGNED

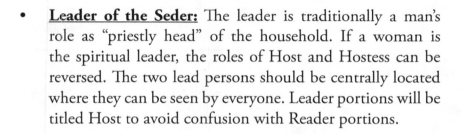

- **Leader of the Seder:** The leader is traditionally a man's role as "priestly head" of the household. If a woman is the spiritual leader, the roles of Host and Hostess can be reversed. The two lead persons should be centrally located where they can be seen by everyone. Leader portions will be titled Host to avoid confusion with Reader portions.

The leader will identify other participants to read or fill other roles, which are listed below. Preferably these people can be identified or selected in advance to facilitate the smooth flow of events, but if not, these persons can be asked to volunteer during the event itself. All readings can be redirected if preferred by the leader, family, or community sponsoring the Seder.

The leader will be: _____

- **Hostess:** This is usually a married leader's spouse (or a spiritually mature person). Aside from lighting the candles on the head table, certain portions in this Haggadah have been delegated to give her a sizable role.

The hostess will be: _____

- **Table heads:** Preferably one man and one woman (or couple) per table to help with the leadership responsibilities at each table.

  Table heads will be:
  - _____

  - _____

  - _____

- **Person 1, 2, and 3:** If you know of strong readers who will be present, assign these portions to them in advance. They include longer text portions, as well as sections with Hebrew words or names to pronounce. Good readers will make the Seder move smoothly and be more enjoyable to the listeners.

  Persons 1, 2, and 3 will be:
  - _____

  - _____

  - _____

- **Volunteer readers:** The Passover is supposed to include everyone's participation. Shorter, easy-to-read sections can be given to guests at the Seder who raise their hands to volunteer. Table leaders will start at one side of the room and have everyone at that table read, then move to the next table. (If you do this, it's important to let your guests know they can pass if they're uncomfortable reading aloud.)

- *Mah nishtanah:* A Hebrew reading of "the four questions" is usually sung or read by the youngest child/adult who knows Hebrew, but can be skipped or just read in English. If someone wants to try doing it, you can go to YouTube sites providing good renditions.

  This child or person will be: _____

- **Intercessor:** This Haggadah includes a prayer for the persecuted today. To include this in your Seder, it is good to have someone close the memorial time with a prayer, either by host, hostess, or a person with a heart for intercession.

  The intercessor will be: _____

- **Servers:** If there is going to be a meal, it is wise to have some delegated servers or volunteers in advance to handle these responsibilities: set up, serving, and clean-up. (Often others will offer to help and can be directed by those in charge.)

Servers will be:

- _____

- _____

- _____

- **<u>Non-designated persons:</u>** There will be readings for all attending—parts specifically for men or women, as well as a question/answer portion between one to four children and one to four parents. It is clearly explained in the context so they can be chosen at that time.

3

CHECKLIST FOR TABLE SETUP

Before the Seder begins, prepare the table(s) in the following manner:

- **Place settings:** Each person should have: one filled glass of water, a glass of wine (or grape juice), a dinner plate, utensils, and two napkins (one for Seder and one for dinner).

- **Haggadot:** Have one book per person (or two can share). Jewish households collect these at the end of the evening to reuse yearly. If leader is doing the Seder as a demonstration, multiple copies are not needed. Leader can instruct guests in areas where they can participate, or use overheads for group readings or songs. Often guests who have never done a Seder before will be interested in taking a Haggadah home to review or share with others. Leaders should decide in advance if they want to make copies available for guests and what cost might be involved.

- **Matzah:** One box of matzah can be placed on each table for the Seder and for snacking.

- **Wine and/or grape juice:** Have enough per table for four 2-4 ounce servings per person.

- **Water pitcher:** At least one per table to allow water glasses to be refilled as needed.

- **Water pitcher or bowl, towels:** Make sure pitcher or bowl is large enough to be used for hand washing. The pitcher or bowl will be passed around the table, along with paper towels for drying. Some Seders provide a basin to wash each other's feet as Messiah did.

- **Salt water:** One half cup per table with enough salt to make the water cloudy.

- **Two candlesticks, candles, matches:** These can be put on each table or just the head table.

- **A Seder plate:** One plate on each table with food items 1–7 below. If you are looking for memorable Seder plates to use yearly, they can be found in stores selling Jewish items or online. You can use reusable plastic or paper Seder plates as well. A Seder plate can also be made by simply separating items on a large dinner plate. Here are the items:

  1. **Parsley (*karpas*):** Enough to provide a sprig for each person at the table.

  2. **Lamb shank bone (*z'roa*):** Ask a butcher at your food market for this if you can't find one.

3. **Charoset:**[1] This is a mixture made of apples, cinnamon, walnuts, honey, and red wine (or grape juice)—at least one tablespoon per person.

4. **Horseradish root (or ginger):** One piece to hold up.

5. **Bitter herb (*maror*):** Ground horseradish, enough for each person to dip in twice.

6. **Roasted eggs (*beitzah*):** or brown egg, one per plate.

7. **Unleavened bread (*matzah*):** Break matzot into quarters and put one per person at the table on the Seder plate.

---

1 See Section 1 Chapter 4 for charoset recipe.

- **Optional table elements:** Salt and pepper, bowl of hard-boiled eggs, extra charoset to eat with the matzot on the table, mixed nuts, etc., to ease hunger during the Seder.

The head table should also include the following items:

- <u>**Unity bag (*matzah tash*):**</u> This is a three-pocket matzah cover with an *Afikomen* container inside. The Unity bag is placed by the leader to be used at a designated time in the Seder. Since the destruction of the Temple and lack of a Passover lamb sacrifice, this has become a focal part of the Seder. Fill each of the three pockets with one whole piece of matzah prior to the Seder. It is called a "Unity bag" because it unites the three matzot into "one element." The smaller *Afikomen* holder is left empty and placed inside. "*Afikomen*" is a Greek word meaning "to come." Later in the Seder it will be filled with a portion of a piece of matzah from the Unity bag and will be explained at that time. (For those who believe our Messiah came and is "to come" again, it will have even greater significance.)

The traditional Unity bag and *Afikomen* sets were white and square. Modern ones are often colorful, decorative, and sometimes round. They can be bought or easily made.

To see what these items look like, go online and search for three-pocket matzah covers and *Afikomen* bags.

Below are instructions for making a permanent set that can be sewn and decorated as a keepsake to use again or a simple makeshift model to be used once.

1. Keepsake Unity bag and *Afikomen* holder: Requires five cloth (linen) napkins or material of equal size

(preferably one white for the *Afikomen*). Matzah holder: Sew four napkins/cloths together on three sides to form a container with three pockets; the fourth side is left open to place the matzah. *Afikomen* holder: fold the fifth (white) napkin/cloth into fourths to form a rectangle or square. Sew on three sides, leaving one side open for the *Afikomen*, which is a broken half to two-thirds of a piece of matzah. (The open side can be folded over to form a flap like an envelope. The empty napkin is tucked into the Unity bag before the Seder.) Children (or adults) can decorate them with fabric paints, lace, and other craft items, as seen online.

2. A simple Unity bag can be made using one large linen napkin or hand towel. Center three whole matzot along the upper edge of the cloth. Use two square paper towels or pieces of wax paper to put between the matzot as dividers. Take a separate smaller white cloth or dinner napkin and fold it in with the matzot to be used later as the *Afikomen* holder. Fold over the sides of the outer linen napkin to enclose the bundle of matzot, creating a Unity bag.

- **Cup of Elijah:** Additional filled wine cup in front of an empty chair.

- **Pillow or cushion:** To be placed by the side of the leader of the Seder as a symbol or reminder to recline and relax, as one who is free.

4

PASSOVER MENU AND RECIPES

To fully experience the Passover, one would serve an unleavened meal like the one the Messiah celebrated with His disciples at His Last Supper. (Leaven in Scripture represents sin.) A traditional Passover menu consists of the courses described below. Some of the traditional recipes have also been included.

- Appetizer: Gefilte fish (available online or at stores selling Jewish items).
- Soup: Chicken soup with matzah balls.
- Main course: According to Ashkenazi (Eastern European) tradition, chicken, beef brisket, or any beef will do. Those who follow the Sephardic (Spanish, Portuguese) tradition still eat lamb as is the biblical mandate. Messianic Seders go either way.
- Side dishes: Salad, vegetables, potatoes, rice dishes, matzah kugels.
- Desserts: Passover sponge cake, honey cake, and macaroon cookies are good options for purchase or baking. Also fruits, sherbet, or plain ice cream.

Recipes

Charoset is the only required recipe. as it is used in the Seder. All other recipes are merely suggestions based on traditional Jewish dishes passed down by our families.

Charoset
(for Mortar- Required)
A traditional recipe
Serves 8-10

12 apples, diced (peeled or unpeeled)
3 cups chopped walnuts
4 tablespoon honey (or brown sugar)
3 teaspoon cinnamon
9 tablespoon sweet red wine (or grape juice)

Blend items together well, or use a food processor, until mixture is well blended (resembling mortar). Cover and refrigerate.

Note: For those with allergies, make some without nuts or substitute golden raisins.

Snacks During Passover Seder or Demonstrations
Snacks to ease hunger can be placed on Seder tables, or served as refreshments at a Passover demonstration. Good options include: more hard-boiled or deviled eggs, charoset or hummus with matzot, vegetables and dip, fruits, nuts, and unleavened sweets.

Chicken Matzah Ball Soup

Soup:

Any chicken soup recipe or prepared chicken broth/stock. (Can add cut carrots, celery, onion, parsnip and dill to enhance the flavor.)

Matzah balls:

Makes approximately 12 balls

4 large eggs
2 tablespoons chicken fat or cooking oil
¼ cup seltzer or chicken broth
1 cup matzah meal
Salt and white or ground pepper to taste
Garlic and onion powder to taste (optional)

Beat eggs well with a fork. Mix in all other ingredients but seasonings. Add seasonings to taste. Mold into a cohesive ball (mass), then cover and refrigerate several hours (or overnight).

How to make matzah balls: dip hands into mixture and form them the size of golf balls (use cold water to clean hands if mixture is too sticky), drop balls into soup and bring to a slow boil, then cover and simmer about 30 minutes until they are soft and rise to the top.

Main Dish

The typical main dishes are beef brisket (see below) and chicken, but any dish except pork will work. Any ingredients are OK, except leaven. Often matzah meal is used for recipes instead of flour. Here's an example of a main dish you might enjoy preparing:

Beef Brisket
Eisen family recipe
Serves 8

One 5-pound brisket of beef
4 cups sliced onions
2 teaspoon salt (sea salt or regular)
1 teaspoon fresh ground black pepper
1 cup barbecue sauce or ketchup
3 tablespoons brown sugar
1 teaspoon garlic powder

First arrange onions on bottom of roasting pan to cushion the beef. Season brisket with salt, pepper, then place meat on top of onions. Combine barbecue sauce or ketchup, brown sugar and garlic powder and pour ingredients over brisket. Cover pan with foil and bake at 350 degrees for 2 1/2 hours. Remove foil cover and bake another 30 minutes until tender. Let cool for 5-10 minutes then put on a carving board to slice. Be sure to cut across the grain of the beef.

Side Dishes

Carrot and Sweet Potato Tzimmes
Affrime family recipe
Serves 8-10

2 large sweet potatoes
1 ½ pounds carrots
3 tablespoons butter
½ teaspoon salt
1 cup water
½ cup raisins
1 cup prunes (pitted)
3/4 cup dried apricots
6 tablespoons brown sugar
½ tablespoon cinnamon
¼ tablespoon cloves
1 tablespoon lemon juice
1 grated orange peel
2 tablespoons honey

Peel and slice carrots and sweet potatoes into ⅛-inch slices. Melt butter in a large saucepan and sauté both for 5 minutes each. Place each aside. Add all remaining ingredients to saucepan and boil for 2–3 minutes until everything seems to be combined well. Use a casserole dish or disposable aluminum 3-inch deep trays. Mix layers of carrots and sweet potatoes and then the fruits and spices. Continue making layers as needed. Cover pan or pans and bake for 2 hours in a 350 F oven. If too soupy, bake uncovered for 20 more minutes at 325 F.

Israeli Salad
Affrime family recipe
Serves 8-10

6 cups diced tomatoes
6 cups diced cucumber
2 cup diced red and/or yellow peppers
1 1/2 cup finely chopped parsley
1 cup diced red onion
6 tablespoons fresh lemon juice
6 tablespoons extra virgin olive oil
Himalayan or sea salt to taste
Ground black pepper to taste
Optional: 3/4 - 1 cup finely chopped mint or cilantro

Cut tomatoes, cucumbers, and peppers into small ¼–½-inch cubes.
Combine all ingredients together in a large bowl. Season with salt
and pepper to taste. Refrigerate at least 2–3 hours until chilled before
serving.

Passover Matzah Kugel

(This recipe can also be used as chicken stuffing)
Eisen family recipe
Serves 8

4 grated carrots
4 celery stalks - diced into small pieces
2 large grated onions
1 1/2 cup water
1/2 teaspoon salt and pepper (or to taste)
1 dry package of chicken gravy mix
2 tablespoon melted butter or margarine
2 cup matzah meal
5 beaten eggs
2 grated potatoes
2 tablespoon dill

Boil carrots, onions, and diced celery in the water. Add salt, pepper and packet of gravy mix. Cook until water is absorbed. Add butter, matzah meal, eggs, raw grated potatoes and dill. Preheat oven to 350 degrees. Generously grease a baking pan. Bake until firm and golden brown (usually 45 minutes).

Apple Matzo Kugel

Affrime family recipe
Serves 12–15

8 pieces of matzot
6 eggs, beaten well (to make fluffier, beat whites first and fold in yolks)
1 cup light brown sugar (raw or white can be used)
½ cup coconut oil (canola or sunflower oil)
1 tablespoon ground cinnamon
½ teaspoon salt
4 large peeled apples (cut into small pieces)
¾-1 cup golden raisins (for variation: use ½ raisins, ½ craisins)

Preheat oven to 350 F. Grease a large baking dish or two medium square baking dishes.

Run matzot under hot water until soft, then break into small pieces in a medium-sized bowl.

In a large bowl, mix together eggs, sugar, oil, cinnamon, and salt. Add matzah and mix well.

Fold in apples and raisins. Spoon mixture into greased baking dish and spread evenly.

Bake 50–60 minutes or until nicely browned. (Use toothpick to assure apples are well cooked.)

Desserts

Coconut Macaroons
Makes 48 cookies

1 package (14 ounce) or 5 ⅓ cups flaked coconut
1 can (14 ounce) sweetened condensed milk
2 teaspoons vanilla extract
1 teaspoon almond extract
(*For chocolate macaroons, stir ¼ cup semi-sweet chocolate mini morsels into dough*)

Preheat oven to 350° F. Grease baking sheets. Combine coconut, sweetened condensed milk, vanilla extract, and almond extract in large bowl. Drop a teaspoonful on prepared baking sheets; press each cookie lightly with back of spoon. Bake 10–14 minutes or until lightly browned around edges. Immediately remove from baking sheets to wire racks to cool. Store loosely covered at room temperature.

Aunt Sandra's Passover Sponge Cake

Affrime family recipe

10 eggs (at room temperature 24 hours prior)
2 cups sugar
¼ teaspoon salt
1 cup cake meal
Juice of 2 oranges and 1 lemon to make 4 ounces (fruit must be at room temp. 24 hours prior)
⅓ cup potato starch

Spray or grease a 10-inch bundt pan and set aside. Preheat oven to 350 F. In large bowl, beat eggs until very firm (don't separate). Pour in sugar slowly until absorbed. Add salt to mix until absorbed, then cake meal, then juice until absorbed, and lastly potato starch. Pour mixed batter into bundt pan and bake for 50–55 minutes. Cool thoroughly on wire rack. Use thin spatula to loosen from pan before removing.

5

OTHER DETAILS

Hiding the *Afikomen*

There is a portion in the Seder known as "Breaking of the Middle Matzah" when the *Afikomen* is placed in the container to be hidden sometime during the meal. The host or a designated person hides it, making sure the children are not watching. After the meal, the children are sent to look for it. The host will also need to inform the children when to begin searching, which usually is during dessert time or right afterward, when transitioning back to the Seder. The child who finds the *Afikomen* brings it to the host and is rewarded with $1–$5. This is done when the second portion of the Seder begins.

Worship

The transition periods before and after the meal offer an opportunity for worship music either by a worship team or group participation. Lyrics can be set up on an overhead projector, or a song sheet can be handed out with the Haggadot. Including a worship segment while transitioning to and from the meal will add enjoyment to the evening.

The following is a list of songs that have traditionally been a part of the Seder; the lyrics are included in the body of the book. If you want to include them, below is a list of YouTube links where they can be heard. They are listed in the order you will find them.

"Four Questions: Ma Nishtanah"— Jewish Holiday Songs

"Dayenu: It Would Have Been Enough"— BimBam

"The Horse and Rider: I Will Sing Unto the Lord" (Exodus 15)—Lifetree Kids

"Eliyahu HaNavi: Elijah the Prophet Song"— Shaboom

"L'Shanah Haba'ah: Next Year in Jerusalem"— Jewish Holiday Songs

The following songs work thematically into the Seder, or you may have your own preferences. We use one of the following during the hand-washing ceremony:

"Make Me a Servant" written and recorded by Kelly Willard

"Give Us Clean Hands" written by Charlie Hall and recorded by Mark Schultz

"Humble Yourself" written by Kelly Willard and recorded by Maranatha

We usually play one or two slower, relaxing songs in the transition period to serving dinner, then one or two livelier songs after the meal to energize and transition back to the Seder.

Songs before the meal:

"Song of Moses" written and recorded by Paul Wilbur

"Eternally Grateful" recorded by Susan Mendelson and Liberated Wailing Wall

"Lamb of God" written and recorded by Marty Goetz

"Lamb of God" written and recorded by Twila Paris

"By Your Blood" written by Alan Grandon, Jeff Hamlin and recorded by Paul Wilbur

"Worthy is the Lamb" written and recorded by Darlene Zschech

Songs following the meal:

"Great and Wonderful" written by Durham, M.W Smith and recorded by Maranatha

"Hinei Mah Tov" Psalm 133 (traditional Jewish song easily found online)

"My Redeemer Lives" written by Reuben Morgan and recorded by Maranatha

"You Are My Salvation" written by Joel Chernoff and recorded by Lamb

How much time to allow for the evening

The Haggadah portion of the evening, if done smoothly with strong readers, can take up to two hours in its entirety. This timeframe can vary if portions are skipped, more worship is included, or you're waiting on readers to volunteer.

If a full meal is offered, it can take another hour or more to include serving, eating, and transitioning. When clearing tables after the dinner, make sure to leave wine glasses and the wine or grape juice on the tables.

Whether or not you do the entire Seder or skip portions can be a decision made in advance, or can be adjusted during the course of the evening, as the leader chooses.

This Haggadah presents eight events during the evening, starting with a "Welcome" and ending with a section called "Return to the Seder" which follows the Passover meal. I highly recommend that Seder leaders read through this entire Haggadah in advance, so they can be familiar with its contents.

I also suggest that, as you read through this Haggadah ahead of time, you mark sections you feel are essential, and some you may feel are less essential. Having sections marked in advance will help you shift gears if the evening goes long. It will help you avoid sacrificing key components so that participants can glean a true appreciation for the Passover and its implications in the Last Supper. (In our personal experience, we've never had anyone—even unbelievers or newcomers to the Seder— participate and not enjoy the entire evening).

2 PARTICIPATING IN THE PASSOVER SEDER

ORDER OF EVENTS FOR THE PASSOVER SEDER

STEP 1

WELCOME

HOST: Passover, or Pesach, is the world's oldest known instituted religious festival that is still celebrated today, as well as the most familiar and universally observed Jewish Holy Day. God instituted it through His servant Moses circa 1446 BC. Families gather yearly to retell of the miraculous events performed for their ancestors by a Sovereign God who had made a covenant with their forefathers: Abraham, Isaac, and Jacob. This evening we will recall the history of our ancestors' deliverance from bondage in Egypt, and the beginning of their history as a nation consecrated by God to be holy, or "set apart."

ALL: *"For I am the LORD that brought you up out of the land of Egypt, to be your God; ye shall therefore be holy, for I am holy."* **Leviticus 11:45 JPS**

HOST: Passover is unique, as participants are to let their hearts, minds, and senses engage as if we ourselves had emerged from Egypt! Thousands of Haggadot (the plural form of Haggadah, which means "The Telling") have been published since this tradition began in the mid-1500s. They arrange the historical events of Israel's deliverance into a Seder, which means "order." Seders include both the story and a meal, as we pay tribute to our Hebrew ancestors' last supper the night before leaving Egypt. Pages 27 and 28 provide the sequence of the Seder. Passover is the first of seven yearly Appointed Seasons of the LORD given to God's people to commemorate.

ALL: "*These are the appointed seasons of the LORD, even holy convocations, which ye shall proclaim in their appointed season. In the first month, on the fourteenth day of the month at dusk, is the LORD's passover.*" **Leviticus 23:4–5 JPS**

HOSTESS: The Scriptures refer to these occasions as *moed* (מועד), meaning an "appointed time, place, meeting or season," although usually interpreted as a "feast." While both the Jewish and Christian traditions often interpret them as the Feasts of the Jews, the Holy Scriptures specifically call them the Appointed Seasons of יהוה׳ (YHVH), translated "LORD." There are seven specific times a year that God commands His Covenant people to keep appointments which He has made to gather with them. The personal name of God is used in calling these gatherings, the very name that God uses to introduce Himself to Moses in Exodus 3, and commanded Moses to teach the Israelites. It is a direct invitation from God to know and be known in a personal way, as did our forefathers. In order to discern when God is using His personal name, the rest of this Haggadah replaces "LORD" with the English consonants "YHVH" substituted for the Hebrew letters. Since ancient Hebrew manuscripts rarely included vowels in their writings, God's personal name has been pronounced several different ways: Yehovah, Jehovah, Yahveh and Yahweh. Using just the consonants will allow you, the reader, the opportunity to choose the pronunciation you prefer.[2]

ALL: "And God said moreover unto Moses: *'Thus shalt thou say unto the children of Israel: YHVH, the God of your fathers, the God of Abraham, the God of Isaac, and the God of Jacob, hath sent me unto you; this is My name for ever, and this is My memorial unto all generations.'* " **Exodus 3:15 JPS**

PERSON 1: "And YHVH spoke unto Moses, saying: *'Speak unto Aaron and unto his sons, saying: On this wise ye shall bless the children of Israel; ye shall say unto them: YHVH bless thee, and keep thee; YHVH make His face to shine upon thee, and be gracious unto thee; YHVH lift up His countenance upon thee, and give thee peace.*[3] *So shall they put My name upon the children of Israel, and I will bless them.'* " **Numbers 6:24-27 JPS**

HOST: All Haggadot include the elements you see on the table, which are usually shared in a common order, but they vary considerably in length, design, and additional content. As with some Haggadot, this one offers some speculation as to how and when the Seder traditions may have originated. As a Messianic Haggadah, it also includes the typologies of the Spring Appointed Seasons of YHVH given to Israel (Leviticus

---

2   Modern Hebrew has neither the "J" nor "W" sound; and more recently found ancient manuscripts favor the reading "Yehovah". For more information see Section 3 Chapter 6.

3   These verses are known as "The Aaronic Benediction", which is still spoken over the Jewish people by their rabbis today at the end of the service.

23), and their greater fulfillment in Messiah Yeshua's life, death, and resurrection. Yeshua, meaning "salvation," is Jesus' actual Hebrew name. "Christ" refers to His title as "The Messiah" or "HaMashiach," meaning "the Anointed" in Hebrew. The Hebrew translated to English, Yeshua the Messiah, will be utilized for the Seder.

This Haggadah also includes some information not normally found in most traditional Rabbinic or Messianic Haggadot:

1. a plethora of biblical references from the Hebrew Scriptures (Tanakh) and New Covenant (*B'rit Hadashah*)

2. an account from Genesis explaining God's promise to Abraham and his family

3. the typology in Joseph's and Moses's lives foreshadowing aspects of Messiah's life

4. a section in the back giving further information split into five subjects mentioned in the Seder, for those interested in a more in-depth understanding.

We hope this evening demonstrates why celebrating Passover is and should be important to Christians as well as Jews, as they see the relevance of the Appointed Seasons in proclaiming Messiah. Come join Him at the Seder!

PERSON 2: *"So don't let anyone pass judgment on you in connection with eating and drinking, or in regard to a Jewish festival or New Moon or Shabbat. These are a shadow of things that are coming, but the body is of the Messiah."* **Colossians 2:16–17 CJB**

STEP 2

CANDLE LIGHTING AND BLESSINGS

HOSTESS: Traditionally, Shabbat and the Holy Days begin with the woman of the house lighting candles and saying a prayer. Day begins at sundown (Genesis 1), so the candle-lighting marks the beginning of the day of Passover. The glow of the candles reminds us that God is always present, lighting our path both physically and spiritually. As Messianic believers, we are reminded that Messiah came into the world through a woman to give us spiritual light.

MEN: *"The sun shall be no more thy light by day, neither for brightness shall the moon give light unto thee; but YHVH shall be unto thee an everlasting light, and thy God thy glory."*
Isaiah 60:19 JPS

WOMEN: "Yea, He saith: *'It is too light a thing that thou shouldest be My servant to raise up the tribes of Jacob, and to restore the offspring of Israel; I will also give thee for a light of the nations, that My salvation may be unto the end of the earth.'"* **Isaiah 49:6 JPS**

(Hostess lights the candles and recites the prayers. All Hebrew prayers are transliterated for anyone who wants to join in the Hebrew readings. All can join in with the English.)

בָּרוּךְ אַתָּה יְהוָה אֱלֹהֵינוּ מֶלֶךְ הָעוֹלָם, אֲשֶׁר קִדְּשָׁנוּ בְּמִצְוֹתָיו וּבִשְׁמוֹ אָנוּ מַדְלִיקִים נֵרוֹת שֶׁל יוֹם טוֹב אָמֵן

HOSTESS: *Baruch atah YHVH Eloheinu Melech ha-olom, asher kidshanu b'mitzvo-tav, uu-vishmo anu madlikim neyrot shel yom tov.* Amen.

ALL: Blessed are You, YHVH our God, King of the Universe, who hast set us apart by Thy commandments, and in whose Name we kindle the festival lights. Amen.

FOLLOWING PRAYER:

בָּרוּךְ אַתָּה יְהוָה אֱלֹהֵינוּ מֶלֶךְ הָעוֹלָם, שֶׁהֶחֱיָנוּ וְקִיְמָנוּ וְהִגִּיעָנוּ לַזְּמַן הַזֶּה. אָמֵן

HOSTESS: *Baruch atah YHVH Eloheinu Melech ha-olom, she-hecheyanu v'ki-yemanu v'higianu lazeman hazeh.* Amen.

ALL: Blessed are You, YHVH, our God, King of the Universe, who hast kept us in life and preserved us, and enables us to reach this season. Amen.

STEP 3

PREPARING FOR PASSOVER

SEARCH FOR LEAVEN – "BEDIKAT KHAMEYTZ"

HOST: Preparing for the Passover season includes thoroughly cleansing the home of anything containing leaven, a ritual called "bedikat khameytz" (search for leaven). Religious households take this tradition very seriously as leaven makes bread ferment and rise; likewise, the sin of pride corrupts and puffs us up. In spiritual preparation we are to search our hearts and repent of any sinful ways. According to rabbinic custom, the home is cleansed of leaven prior to the Passover to make us "worthy" of the Seder. Yet in Scripture, God commands the Hebrews to remove the leaven from their homes the morning after the Seder (Passover day) to commemorate the seven days of Unleavened Bread. We do not believe God expected His people to merit His favor, but rather offers it as a gift of grace, lovingkindness, and faithfulness to Abraham and his offspring.

MEN: *"And I will make of thee, Abraham, a great nation, and I will bless thee, and make thy name great; and be thou a blessing.*

And I will bless them that bless thee, and him that curseth thee will I curse; and in thee shall all the families of the earth be blessed." **Genesis 12:2–3 JPS**

WOMEN: *"And he (Abraham) believed in YHVH; and He counted it to him for righteousness."* **Genesis 15:6 JPS**

PERSON 3: *"And ye shall observe the Feast of Unleavened Bread; for in this same day have I brought your hosts out of the land of Egypt; therefore shall ye observe this day throughout your generations by an ordinance forever. In the first month, on the fourteenth day of the month at evening, ye shall eat unleavened bread, until the one and twentieth day of the month at evening. Seven days shall there be no leaven found in your houses; for whosoever eateth that which is leavened, that soul shall be cut off from the congregation of Israel, whether he be a sojourner, or one that is born in the land."* **Exodus 12:17–19 JPS**

HOSTESS: Showing trust by obedience to YHVH that evening in Egypt, Jews as well as Gentiles smeared the blood of a Pesach lamb upon their doorways. The unleavened bread on our Seder table represents the unblemished lambs that died so that "death passed over" their homes. It also commemorates the perfection of God. His people were to respond in gratitude for God's covenant love and deliverance by leaving behind *"the leaven of Egypt."*

ALL: *"And ye shall be unto Me a kingdom of priests, and a holy nation. These are the words which thou shalt speak unto the children of Israel."* **Exodus 19:6 JPS**

HOST: The Hebrew number for completeness is *"sheva,"* or seven. As we celebrate the seven-day Feast of Unleavened Bread, we can ask His help to reveal and remove "leaven" from our lives, not only our homes.

ALL: *"Search me, O God, and know my heart, try me, and know my thoughts; And see if there be any way in me that is grievous, and lead me in the way everlasting."* **Psalm 139:23–24 JPS**

THE SEDER PLATE

PERSON 1: "Speak ye unto all the congregation of Israel, saying: *In the tenth day of this month they shall take to them every man a lamb, according to their fathers' houses, a lamb for a household; and if the household be too little for a lamb, then shall he and his neighbor next unto his house take one according to the number of the souls; according to every man's eating ye shall make your count for the lamb. Your lamb shall be without blemish, a male of the first year; ye shall take it from the sheep, or from the goats; and ye shall*

keep it unto the fourteenth day of the same month; and the whole assembly of the congregation of Israel shall kill it at dusk. And they shall take of the blood, and put it on the two side-posts and on the lintel, upon the houses wherein they shall eat it. And they shall eat the flesh in that night, roast with fire, and unleavened bread; with bitter herbs they shall eat it. Eat not of it raw, nor sodden at all with water, but roast with fire; its head with its legs and with the inwards thereof. And ye shall let nothing of it remain until the morning; but that which remaineth of it until the morning ye shall burn with fire. And thus shall ye eat it: with your loins girded, your shoes on your feet, and your staff in your hand; and ye shall eat it in haste—it is YHVH's passover. For I will go through the land of Egypt in that night, and will smite all the first-born in the land of Egypt, both man and beast; and against all the gods of Egypt I will execute judgments: I am YHVH. And the blood shall be to you for a token upon the houses where ye are; and when I see the blood, I will pass over you, and there shall no plague be upon you to destroy you, when I smite the land of Egypt."
Exodus 12:3–13 JPS

(The host holds up each item as it is introduced. Table leaders can do the same.)

HOST: Rabbi Gamaliel, a contemporary of Yeshua, said: "He who does not speak forth these three essentials of the Passover Seder has not discharged his duty." They are:

- The shank bone: The bone of a lamb representing the sacrifice eaten at their last supper in Egypt.

- Maror: This bitter herb on the Seder plate is whole, as well as crushed to partake of with matzah in our Seder. It should cause tears as we recall our ancestors' years of slavery.
- Matzah: To make this unleavened bread, the dough must be carefully kneaded, striped, and pierced, then baked in less than eighteen minutes to prevent it from rising.

The following items have been traditionally added to the Seder:

- Karpas: Parsley was added to represent the hyssop our forefathers used to smear the lamb's blood upon the doors of their homes. It also reminds us that this is the beginning of the spring season, when the Earth brings forth new life, and when our people sprang up as a new nation to begin new lives.
- Charoset: This is an apple, walnut, cinnamon, honey, and grape juice (or wine) mixture that is to remind us of the appearance of mortar used by our ancestors to make bricks for Pharaoh. It is sweet to the taste to remind us of their hope for freedom.
- Roasted egg: The roasted egg has been added to the Seder, but it is unclear when or how. We will offer some reasons for this element later in the Seder.

FOUR CUPS OF WINE

PERSON 2: The Seder includes four cups of wine. The Torah does not refer to it as an element of the Passover, yet it has become one of the focal elements of the Seder. It is said to represent the four *"I wills"* God proclaims to Moses in Exodus 6:6–7. Each time we refill our glasses, we will recite the biblical portion assigned to it and share the significance of that particular cup. If your first cup is not already filled, please fill it at this time.

STEP 4

THE PASSOVER SEDER

FIRST CUP OF WINE: SANCTIFICATION – "KIDDUSH CUP"

ALL: *"Wherefore say unto the children of Israel: I am YHVH, and I will bring you out from under the burdens of the Egyptians."* **Exodus 6:6a JPS**

HOST: This first cup is the Kiddush cup, meaning "sanctification." It reminds us that our ancestors were not only to come out of slavery, but also to leave behind the carnal ways of the Egyptians to be His people and He their Lord God and Master. To identify with our ancestors in their newly found freedom, we lean to the left when partaking of the Seder elements in a symbolic gesture of reclining at the meal—an unknown luxury for a slave! Hold up the first cup of wine as the blessing is said to give praise to Adonai for our ancestors' freedom, as well as ours today.

HOST: We say: *Baruch atah YHVH, Eloheinu Melech ha-olom, borey p'ri hagafen.* Amen.

בָּרוּךְ אַתָּה יְהוָה אֱלֹהֵינוּ מֶלֶךְ הָעוֹלָם, בּוֹרֵא פְּרִי הַגָּפֶן. אָמֵן

ALL: Blessed are You, YHVH our God, King of the Universe, who creates the fruit of the vine. Amen.

(All lean left and partake of the first cup.)

HOSTESS: Leaving Egypt and "being set apart from the nations" did not change their human nature and the human heart's propensity to rebel, leading to forty years of wandering. Those of us who believe Yeshua was the promised Messiah believe He came to accomplish what the Law could not, by circumcising our hearts and freeing us to live holy lives (though sadly we still often choose to follow our own ways). The "Last Supper" was actually the Passover meal Yeshua celebrated with His disciples before His death. He took a cup of wine from the table to symbolize the atoning sacrifice He would make by offering up His sinless life and blood, like that of the Pesach Lamb on their dinner plates, so judgment could "pass over" them.

ALL: *"For the life of the flesh is in the blood; and I have given it to you upon the altar to make atonement for your souls; for it is the blood that maketh atonement by reason of the life."*
Leviticus 17:11 JPS

MEN: *"Moreover YHVH your God will circumcise your heart and the heart of your descendants, to love YHVH your God with all your heart and with all your soul, so that you may live."*
Deuteronomy 30:6 JPS

WOMEN: *"Therefore, if anyone is united with the Messiah, he is a new creation—the old has passed; look, what has come is fresh and new!"* **2 Corinthians 5:17 CJB**

WASHING OF HANDS – "URCHATZ"

HOSTESS: Each table has a water bowl and hand towels. Washing one's hands signifies a desire for cleanliness of body and soul, as evidenced by the water rituals of the Levitical priests.

ALL: *"Who shall ascend into the mountain of YHVH? And who shall stand in His holy place? He that hath clean hands, and a pure heart; who hath not taken My name in vain, and hath not sworn deceitfully."* **Psalm 24:3–4 JPS**

PERSON 3: Customarily in ancient times, a lowly servant was appointed the task of washing the dirty feet of arriving travelers. At Messiah's last Passover, we see Him reversing the worldly paradigm of leadership and servanthood: humbly kneeling before each of His disciples and washing their feet, then commanding them to do likewise.

ALL: *"Now if I, the Lord and Rabbi, have washed your feet, you also should wash each other's feet. For I have set you an example, so that you may do as I have done to you."* **John 13:14-15 CJB**

HOST: To demonstrate this example of service, table leaders should set the water bowl where the person on their left can dip their fingers; then leaders take a towel and dry their hands. The person whose hands were just cleansed will do likewise for the person to their left until the last person has dried the hands of their table leader.

(During this ceremonial hand washing worshipful music can be played. See suggestions in Section 1, page 24)

DIPPING OF THE PARSLEY – "KARPAS"

(Table leaders should begin passing the parsley and bowl of salt water for dipping around their tables.)

HOST: Parsley represents the hyssop plant used to smear the blood of the lamb upon the doorposts and lintels of the households in Egypt. Both Jews and Gentiles who believed God's warning and obeyed were spared from the tenth and final plague. Hyssop is also mentioned by King David in Psalm 51 as being a symbol of God's cleansing him from the punishment of death for his sin of adultery.

ALL: *"Be gracious unto me, O God, according to Thy mercy; according to the multitude of Thy compassions blot out my transgressions. Wash me thoroughly from mine iniquity and cleanse me from my sin... Purge me with hyssop, and I shall be clean; wash me, and I shall be whiter than snow."* **Psalm 51:3–4, 9 JPS**

PERSON 1: The saltiness of the dipped parsley should not only remind us of the tears of sorrow our ancestors shed in Egypt, but also of the tears of joy the Israelites must have shed after God safely led them through the salty Red Sea! How fitting that their deliverance came in the month of Nissan, or Aviv (meaning "spring"), when winter's barrenness gives way to spring's greenery and the Earth brings forth new life. Likewise, our ancestors "sprang forth" as a new nation in hopes of being "rooted" in the Promised Land! This month would be designated as the beginning of a new life and new year!

ALL: "And YHVH spoke unto Moses and Aaron in the land of Egypt, saying: *This month shall be unto you the beginning of months; it shall be the first month of the year to you.*' "
Exodus 12:1–2 JPS

HOST: We say: *Baruch atah YHVH Eloheinu Melech ha-olom, borey p'ri ha-adamah.* Amen.

בָּרוּךְ אַתָּה יְהֹוָה אֱלֹהֵינוּ מֶלֶךְ הָעוֹלָם, בּוֹרֵא פְּרִי הָאֲדָמָ .אָמֵן

ALL: Blessed are You, YHVH our God, King of the Universe, who creates the fruit of the earth. Amen.

(All lean left and partake of the parsley dipped in salt water.)

BREAKING OF THE MIDDLE MATZAH – "YACHATZ"

(Host holds up the unity bag with the three pieces of matzah)

HOST: As leader of the Seder, I am holding up the item that contains the quintessential element on the Passover table since the destruction of the Temple brought an end to the annual sacrifice of the Pesach lambs. This bag is called a Unity bag. It is a container with three pockets, each of which holds a separate whole matzah. The separations make them distinct, yet the bag makes them one unified element. As the family head, I remove this middle matzah from the Unity bag, as well as another folded cloth, which is an *Afikomen* holder. I will now break this middle matzah into two pieces and return the smaller portion to its place in the Unity bag. This larger portion is called the *Afikomen*, a Greek word meaning "to come." Rabbis claim it got its name because it "comes" after the meal as the last food to be eaten. No one can confirm when or how this tradition originated, but it would have been when Greek was the common language of the Jews. Rabbis did not institute it until sometime after the destruction of the Temple in AD 70, when the unleavened matzah replaced the sacrificial lambs as a symbol of sinlessness on the Seder plate.

HOSTESS: While not found in the Jewish Scriptures, Yeshua seemed to have instituted something like this during His last Seder eaten with His disciples the night before he was killed. Our host will hold the *Afikomen* up to the candlelight, and you can see how it is both striped and pierced, which is the only way of removing all leaven from the dough. Likewise, Yeshua was striped by the lashes of the Roman whip, and pierced by a crown of thorns, nails, and a spear, although He was without sin. Our family head will now wrap the *Afikomen* in white cloth to be hidden away for a short time. Likewise, Messiah was wrapped in white cloth for burial and hidden away in a tomb for three days by His Heavenly Father.

HOST: More will be said about this in the portion following the meal when we partake of this *Afikomen*. For now, I want the children to pay close attention to what this *Afikomen* holder looks like, because I am going to hide it. After supper I will define a search area, whether in this room or somewhere else, and I will send the children to try and find it. The child who finds it will bring it to me, and I will buy it from you.

STEP 5

STORY OF PASSOVER –
"MAGGID HA PESACH"

PERSON 2: "Then Moses called for all the elders of Israel, and said unto them: *'Draw out, and take you lambs according to your families, and kill the Passover lamb. And ye shall take a bunch of hyssop, and dip it in the blood that is in the basin, and strike the lintel and the two side-posts with the blood that is in the basin; and none of you shall go out of the door of his house until the morning. For YHVH will pass through to smite the Egyptians; and when He seeth the blood upon the lintel, and on the two side-posts, YHVH will pass over the door, and will not suffer the destroyer to come in unto your houses to smite you. And ye shall observe this thing for an ordinance to thee and to thy sons for ever. And it shall come to pass, when ye be come to the land which YHVH will give you, according as He hath promised, that ye shall keep this service. And it shall come to pass, when your children shall say unto you: What mean ye by this service? That ye shall say: It is the sacrifice of YHVH's Passover, for that He passed over the houses of the children of Israel in Egypt, when He smote the Egyptians, and delivered our houses.'* And the people bowed the head and worshipped. And the children of

Israel went and did so; as YHVH had commanded Moses and Aaron, so did they." **Exodus 12:21–28 JPS**

HOST: It has become a part of our heritage to keep this biblical mandate to observe the Passover throughout our generations. The Lord Himself exhorts us to remind and teach our children their history, which in truth is also "His-Story!"

HOSTESS: As our Creator, God knows it's in our genetics to ask questions and seek answers as to: "Why do we do these things?" Parents were to be prepared to answer those questions, which has led to the following traditions that have become a standard part of the Seder.

FOUR QUESTIONS – "MA NISHTANAH" (OPTIONAL)

(This portion allows the youngest child competent in Hebrew to participate by reciting the four questions. If no child can read Hebrew, let an adult do it, or skip down to the English portion.)

Q: Ma nishtanah halailah hazeh, mikol haleylot?
1) *Shebekhol haleylot, anu okhlin, khameytz umatzah? Halailah hazeh, kulo mat-zah.*
2) *Shebekhol haleylot anu okhlin, she'ar yerakot? Halailah hazeh, mar-or-or.*
3) *Shebekhol haleylot eyn anu matbilin, afilu pa'am ekhat? Halailah hazeh, shtey f'am-im.*
4) *Shebekhol haleylot anu okhlin, beyn yoshevin uveyn mesubin? Halailah hazeh, kulanu mesubin.*

*(Host asks one to four children to read the questions below,
and one to four parents to answer them.)*

HOST: *We ask and answer the question: "Why does tonight differ
from all other nights?"*

CHILD 1: *On all other nights we eat either leavened or unleavened
bread. Why on this night do we eat only matzah, which is unleavened
bread?*

CHILD 2: *On all other nights we eat vegetables and herbs of all
kinds. Why on this night do we eat only bitter herbs?*

CHILD 3: *On all other nights we do not dip our herbs. Why on this
night do we dip twice, in salt water and sweet charoset?*

CHILD 4: *On all other nights we eat sitting as we please. Why on
this night do we eat only in a relaxed position?*

(The selected parents will now answer the children's questions.)

PARENT 1: *We eat only matzot tonight, because when Pharaoh let
our ancestors leave Egypt they fled in great haste, and had no time
to allow the bread to rise. Likewise, God commanded them to leave
behind the "leaven of Egypt," which is symbolic for sin.*

PARENT 2: *We only eat bitter herbs, reminding us that our
forefathers' lives were made very bitter under slavery.*

PARENT 3: *We dip herbs twice: first the parsley in saltwater to remind us of the bitter tears our ancestors shed. Later we will dip the horseradish into charoset to remind us that the sweet hope of deliverance enabled our ancestors to endure.*

PARENT 4: *We recline at the table because it is the privilege of a free person, and as a result of this night our ancestors were set free, as we still are today.*

ALL: *"And it shall be when thy son asketh thee in time to come, saying: What is this? that thou shalt say unto him: By strength of hand YHVH brought us out from Egypt from the house of bondage."*
Exodus 13:14 JPS

FOUR KINDS OF CHILDREN – "Arba'ah Ye'ladim" (Optional)

(Four new volunteers can be chosen, or the same volunteers can read.)

HOSTESS: *The Exodus story is told and retold to each generation, as well as to very different kinds of children. Traditionally, we give examples of four types of children to portray the various ways they might need to learn about their heritage.*

PARENT 1: *Wise children are teachable and enjoy participating, so include them in the story. When they ask about what God has commanded us concerning Pesach, share with them: how God brought us out of Egypt with "His outstretched arm and miracles," then gave us the Torah to obey. Use "us" so they include themselves as part of the community that participated in the Exodus.*

PARENT 2: *Rebellious children will choose to exclude themselves and ask: "Why do you ask me to be involved in this Seder?" They detach from the community and are unwilling to learn. Warn them by saying: "This Seder tells what my God did for me when I came out of Egypt! It appears that if you had been there, you would not have obeyed His command, nor been redeemed, as you show no desire to learn!"*

PARENT 3: *Less experienced children might ask: "What is all this?" They need simpler explanations and instructions. Say to them, "Through great sacrifice and with a Mighty Hand, God redeemed us from slavery in Egypt! It is our duty to remind ourselves by observing these things."*

PARENT 4: *Some children are still too young to inquire. Familiarize them with the story anyway. Say, "This Seder is done because Abba God freed me from Egypt and gave so much to me!" Make it about "you," so as to gain their interest in knowing more about their family heritage as they get older.*

PROMISE TO THE PATRIARCHS

ALL: *"And moreover I have heard the groaning of the children of Israel, whom the Egyptians keep in bondage; and I have remembered My covenant ... and I will bring you in unto the land, concerning which I lifted up My hand to give it to Abraham, to Isaac, and to Jacob; and I will give it you for a heritage: I am YHVH."*
Exodus 6:5, 8 JPS

HOST: To truly understand the Exodus story, we need to know some history on how our ancestors ended up in Egypt in the first place. The first inkling of these events is found in Genesis 15, where God foretells Abraham about the future fate of his descendants. We can see why he is called "the father of our faith," believing in the goodness, faithfulness, and sovereignty of God Almighty despite this foreboding prophecy.

PERSON 3: "And He said unto Abram: *'Know of a surety that thy seed shall be a stranger in a land that is not theirs, and shall serve them; and they shall afflict them four hundred years; and also that nation, whom they shall serve, will I judge; and afterward shall they come out with great substance. But thou shalt go to thy fathers in peace; thou shalt be buried in a good old age. And in the fourth generation they shall come back hither; for the iniquity of the Amorite is not yet full.'* " **Genesis 15:13–16 JPS**

HOSTESS: The details leading up to their stay in Egypt begin with the story of Jacob's sons and their attitude toward their favored brother Joseph. Harboring jealousy and hatred toward him, his older brothers sell him into slavery, then deceive their father into believing he was killed by a wild beast. Joseph suffers injustice in his land of captivity as well, until his gift for interpreting dreams brings him favor with Pharaoh.

PERSON 1: "And Pharaoh said unto his servants: *'Can we find such a one as this, a man in whom the spirit of God is?* And Pharaoh said unto Joseph: *'Forasmuch as God hath shown thee all this, there is none so discreet and wise as thou. Thou shalt be over*

my house, and according unto thy word shall all my people be ruled;
only in the throne will I be greater than thou'... Joseph was thirty
years old when he stood before Pharaoh king of Egypt."
Genesis 41:38–40, 46 JPS

PERSON 2: The famine reached Canaan where Israel (Jacob)
and his family dwelt, so he sent his ten eldest sons to Egypt
to buy grain, unaware that this "Egyptian" ruler was their
brother. Joseph longed to disclose himself to them, but first
tested their hearts and found they were repentant. Their guilt
made them fearful of him, but instead they were welcomed with
unconditional love and tears of joy. Like Abraham, he had faith
in the greater purposes of the Lord God in his trials. Joseph
sent his brothers back to Canaan to gather their families and
belongings then return to Egypt where he could care for them.
Jacob is not at first convinced that his "dead son" is actually a
prince in Egypt!

READER: *"And as for you, ye meant evil against me; but God*
meant it for good, to bring to pass, as it is this day, to save much
people alive." **Genesis 50:20 JPS**

READER: "And God spoke unto Israel in the visions of the night,
and said: *'Jacob, Jacob.'* And he said: *'Here am I.'* And He said:
'I am God, the God of thy father; fear not to go down into Egypt;
for I will there make of thee a great nation.'" **Genesis 46:2–3 JPS**

ALL: *"Thy fathers went down into Egypt with threescore and ten*
persons; and now YHVH thy God hath made thee as the stars of
heaven for multitude." **Deuteronomy 10:22 JPS**

HOST: Most rabbis believe Scripture foreshadows two messiahs: one who will suffer like Joseph, the other to reign like David. As Messianic believers, we interpret these same texts as speaking of one Messiah at "two comings." We see in the life of Joseph a typology of Yeshua:

1. both were not recognized for their calling until age thirty

2. they were favored by their fathers, yet misjudged and hated by jealous brethren

3. their brethren made up a story convincing others they were dead

4. both unjustly suffered and were condemned by Gentile authorities

5. both were first accepted and exalted in Gentile nations as second to the throne

6. they provided for all who came to them seeking help (Jew or Gentile)

7. they never stopped loving and longing for reconciliation with their kindred

8. both display unconditional love and forgiveness when their brothers do repent!

PERSON 3: *"And I will pour upon the house of David, And upon the inhabitants of Jerusalem, The spirit of grace and of supplication; And they shall look unto Me because they have thrust him through; And they shall mourn for him, as one mourneth for his only son,*

And shall be in bitterness for him, as one that is in bitterness for his first-born." **Zechariah 12:10 JPS**

HOSTESS: As God Himself needed to convince disbelieving Israel (Jacob) of the good news that his son Joseph was alive and a ruler in Egypt, likewise God will someday convince disbelieving Israel (the nation) of the Good News that His Son is the Prince of Peace who will rule in Jerusalem! The verse below, a section of Isaiah 9, is the only place in this English Tanakh edition that the writers didn't translate; rather it was transliterated from the Hebrew as: "Pele joez-el-gibbor-Abi-ad-sar-shalom," which leaves question as to what it means. However, at the bottom of the Bible was a footnote that gave the translation. Below, the English translation found in that footnote has been inserted (in bold) to make it easier to read. The following two passages from God's Word describe this "son of Israel" as being more than just a "son of man!"

HOST: *"For a child is born unto us, a son is given unto us; and the government is upon his shoulder; and his name is called **Wonderful, Counselor, Mighty God, Everlasting Father, Prince of Peace.** That the government may be increased, and of peace there be no end, upon the throne of David, and upon his kingdom, to establish it, and to uphold it through justice and through righteousness from henceforth even for ever. The zeal of YHVH of hosts doth perform this."* **Isaiah 9:5–6 JPS**

ALL: *"Who hath ascended up into heaven, and descended? Who hath gathered the wind in his fists? Who hath bound the waters*

in his garment? Who hath established all the ends of the earth? What is his name, and what is his son's name, if thou knowest?"
Proverbs 30:4 JPS

HOST: The Israelites remained in Egypt enjoying Pharaoh's favor until Joseph's death. Genesis closes with Joseph laid out in a coffin awaiting the generation who will take his body back to the Promised Land. Having known of the prophecy given to Abraham, one can only speculate as to why they didn't return to Canaan after the famine, or Joseph's death. Four hundred years will pass before "His-Story," and that of the Hebrews, will continue in the book of Exodus.

READER: "And Joseph said unto his brethren: *'I am about to die; but God will surely remember you, and bring you up out of this land unto the land which He swore to Abraham, to Isaac, and to Jacob.'* And Joseph took an oath of the children of Israel, saying: *'God will surely remember you, and ye shall carry up my bones from hence.'* So Joseph died, being a hundred and ten years old. And they embalmed him, and he was put in a coffin in Egypt."
Genesis 50:24–26 JPS

STORY OF MOSES

READER: The book of Exodus opens following 400 years of prophetic silence. The Pharaoh ruling Egypt had not known Joseph. Fearful of the numbers and strength of the Hebrews he enslaved them, yet they still grew in number so he devised an alternate plan. Pharaoh sent soldiers to seize all the Hebrew male infants and throw them in the Nile.

HOSTESS: One Levite mother hid her newborn son for awhile but soon realized he would be found. She entrusted his fate to YHVH and made a basket to carry him down the Nile. Pharaoh's daughter discovered the helpless child and decided to raise him herself; she named him Moses (Egyptian for "drawn from water"). Her ruling father saw no threat in letting this one Hebrew child live that his daughter had rescued. He would grow up in the palace as a brother to the future reigning Pharaoh of Egypt, who would play an essential part in the Passover story. In God's inimitable way, He spared Moses from the waters meant to kill him, and then hid him in the very household that decreed his death!

PERSON 1: "And it came to pass in those days, when Moses was grown up, that he went out unto his brethren, and looked on their burdens; and he saw an Egyptian smiting a Hebrew, one of his brethren. And he looked this way and that way, and when he saw that there was no man, he smote the Egyptian, and hid him in the sand. And he went out the second day, and, behold, two men of the Hebrews were striving together; and he said to him that did the wrong: *'Wherefore smitest thou thy fellow?'* And he said: *'Who made thee a ruler and a judge over us? Thinkest thou to kill me, as thou didst kill the Egyptian?'* And Moses feared, and said: *'Surely the thing is known.'* Now when Pharaoh heard this thing, he sought to slay Moses. But Moses fled from the face of Pharaoh, and dwelt in the land of Midian." **Exodus 2:11–14 JPS**

HOST: Moses was rejected by his Hebrew kin when he first tried to help them, and forsaking the privileged status he enjoyed in Pharaoh's kingdom, he fled and ended up in Midian, where he married, had two sons, and lived a humble shepherd's life. God would use the next forty years of Moses's life to humble and prepare him for his destiny: to be a prophet, deliverer, and leader of the Israelites. Scripture informs us that forty years passed before God heard His people's groanings and remembered His vow to Abraham. "Remembered" does not mean that God had forgotten His vow, but that now was the time meant to fulfill it. YHVH appeared to Moses in a burning bush and commanded him to return to Egypt and tell his brother Pharaoh: "Let my people go!" Moses informed God that he was a poor speaker and therefore would be unsuitable, but God was undeterred. However, God acquiesced to making his brother Aaron his spokesman.

PERSON 2: *"And thou shalt speak unto him (Aaron), and put the words in his mouth; and I will be with thy mouth, and with his mouth, and will teach you what ye shall do. And he shall be thy spokesman unto the people; and it shall come to pass, that he shall be to thee a mouth, and thou shalt be to him in God's stead. And thou shalt take in thy hand this rod, wherewith thou shalt do the signs."* **Exodus 4:15–17 JPS**

READER: Pharaohs were thought to be gods in the flesh by both their people and themselves, so he was not about to yield to a rival god, especially that of his turncoat brother who left his royal position and killed one of his men for some ungrateful slaves. God foretold Moses that Pharaoh would not relent—that is, until YHVH revealed His almighty power and glory in judgments against Egypt and all their gods—Pharaoh included.

MEN: *"And I know that the king of Egypt will not give you leave to go, except by a mighty hand. And I will put forth My hand, and smite Egypt with all My wonders which I will do in the midst thereof. And after that he will let you go."'* **Exodus 3:19–20 JPS**

HOSTESS: You might be surprised to know that most traditional Haggadot never even mention the name of Moses. Two rabbinic views for this omission are: 1) so we don't exalt and idolize the man Moses rather than God Almighty; and 2) so we do not wait for great leaders when action is needed. Yet the Torah specifically exhorts us to expect another Moses-like prophet whom we must obey. Therefore, it would seem prudent to take this occasion to learn more about him.

WOMEN: *"I will raise them up a prophet from among their brethren, like unto thee (Moses); and I will put My words in his mouth, and he shall speak unto them all that I shall command him. And it shall come to pass, that whosoever will not hearken unto My words which he shall speak in My name, I will require it of him."* **Deuteronomy 18:18–19 JPS**

SECOND CUP OF WINE: PLAGUES – "MAKKOT"

(Cups are filled for the second time.)

ALL: *"I will deliver you from their bondage..."* **Exodus 6:6b JPS**

HOST: With this second cup, we will recount the plagues that YHVH brought upon Egypt to reveal the impotence of Pharaoh and Egypt's other gods. The first three plagues fell upon all in Egypt, so that the "fear of YHVH" might be upon all people, Jews and Gentiles alike. God then made a distinction between Egypt and the Israelites; but despite the ever-increasing display of God's sovereignty and superiority, Pharaoh's heart remained hardened. With the seventh plague, YHVH gave each person in Egypt the opportunity to acknowledge and obey Him, thus sparing them the consequences. These plagues reflect not only God's judgment on Egypt, but His love toward the Egyptian people also. Had God rescued His people in one day, none of the Egyptians would have had the opportunity to see, know, fear, and place their hope in the Hebrews' God! With the tenth plague, each household in Egypt had the chance to decide whom they would worship: Pharaoh or YHVH! With the loss of his own son, Pharaoh finally relented and expelled Moses and his people from the land. As Scripture foretold, they would plunder Egypt.

PERSON 3: "And YHVH said unto Moses: '*Yet one plague more will I bring upon Pharaoh and upon Egypt; afterwards he will let you go hence; when he shall let you go, he shall surely thrust you out* *hence altogether. Speak now in the ears of the people, and let them ask every man of his neighbour, and every woman of her neighbour, jewels of silver, and jewels of gold.'* And YHVH gave the people favour in the sight of the Egyptians. Moreover the man Moses was very great in the land of Egypt, in the sight of Pharaoh's servants, and in the sight of the people." **Exodus 11:1–3 JPS**

HOSTESS: While we celebrate our ancestor's redemption, we also realize it came at a great cost. Therefore, it is incumbent upon us to diminish our joy, or wine, in memory of those who suffered these plagues. We will not drink this cup for a while yet, but as each plague is announced (first in Hebrew then English), dip your pinky finger into the wine and let a drop fall onto your plate. The chart below reveals how these plagues were also meant to show YHVH's sovereignty over their supposed gods.

GOD'S TEN PLAGUES OF JUDGMENT

(Only the name of the plagues are recited. Leader reads Hebrew in first column, while all dip off some wine and recite the English in the second column. The extra information is for personal edification.)

	Transliteration with Hebrew	Plagues in English	Exodus Reference	Affected by the Plagues	Egyptian Gods or Goddesses
1	Dam דם	Blood	7:14-25	Egyptians and Hebrews	Anuket; Hapi; Khnum; Satis; Sobek
2	Ts'farde'ah צפרדע	Frogs	8:1-15	Egyptians and Hebrews	Heh; Heket; Nefertum
3	Kinim כנים	Lice, Gnats	8:16-19	Egyptians and Hebrews	Geb; Nu; Sekhmet
4	Arov ערב	Swarms of Flies	8:20-32	Egyptians	Khepri; Uajyt
5	Dever דבר	Livestock	9:1-7	Egyptians	Hathor; Mnevis, Sothis
6	Sh'chin שחין	Boils	9:8-12	Egyptians	Heka; Imhotep; Serket
7	Barad ברד	Hail	9:13-35	Unbelieving Egyptians	Ba'al; Set; Shu; Tefnut
8	Arbe ארבה	Locusts	10:3-20	Egyptians	Neith; Neper; Sokar
9	Choshech חשך	Darkness	10:21-23	Egyptians	Arum; Atum; Horus; Kauket; Kek; Nut; Ra
10	Macat B'chorot מכת בכורות	Slaying of the Firstborn	11:1, 4-8 12:29-33	Unbelieving Egyptians	Osiris; Isis; Pharaoh; Renenutet; Wadjet

> ## INTERCESSION FOR THE PERSECUTED (OPTIONAL)
>
> **HOST:** *Slavery and oppression still exist in our world today. Human trafficking generates billions of dollars annually on the black market. Let us take a moment to bow our heads and in silence remember them. We invite any of you to call out the name of a country or region where people are being persecuted. Each time a place is called out to God, let us once again dip out some wine to remember them. We will end this memorial time with a prayer of intercession.*
> *(Do not drink the wine.)*
> *(Begin time of prayer—host or designated person*
> *closes with final prayer)*

RED SEA CROSSING

PERSON 1: *"And the children of Israel journeyed from Rameses to Succoth, about six hundred thousand men on foot, beside children. And a mixed multitude went up also with them; and flocks, and herds, even very much cattle"* … *"Now the time that the children of Israel dwelt in Egypt was four hundred and thirty years. And it came to pass at the end of four hundred and thirty years, even the selfsame day it came to pass, that all the host of YHVH went out from the land of Egypt."* **Exodus 12:37–38, 40–41 JPS**

MEN: *" 'And when a stranger shall sojourn with thee, and will keep the Passover to YHVH, let all his males be circumcised, and then let him come near and keep it; and he shall be as one that is born in the land; but no uncircumcised person shall eat thereof. One law shall be to him that is homeborn, and unto the stranger that sojourneth among you.' "* **Exodus 12:48–49 JPS**

HOSTESS: From a small tribe of seventy, they became a nation made up of a mixed multitude of God-fearing people who trusted in Israel's God and made the Exodus with them. YHVH guided them in a pillar of cloud by day and fire by night. But God hardened Pharaoh's heart, so he ordered his army to pursue them, which left them cut off at the Red Sea. Almighty God would now show His awesome power, as His people "passed over" on dry ground!

WOMEN: *"And the waters returned, and covered the chariots, and the horsemen, even all the host of Pharaoh that went in after them into the sea; there remained not so much as one of them. But the children of Israel walked upon dry land in the midst of the sea; and the waters were a wall unto them on their right hand, and on their left."* **Exodus 14:28–29 JPS**

HOST: Drowning Egypt's army and chariots was not a random act by God, but rather brought full circle the judgment due them. As they had planned to wipe out Israel's strength by drowning their sons, so YHVH brought upon them cursing in kind, a pattern seen throughout Israel's history. Moses's deliverance as a baby also revealed a prototype of Israel's deliverance as a newborn nation. As Messianic believers, we see a striking similarity between the lives of Moses and Yeshua:

1. both births were prophetically anticipated

2. ruling monarchs of their day attempted to thwart God's plan by killing all male infants

3. both children escaped death by hiding in Egypt until God called them out of Egypt

4. both left their royal estate and were prepared for ministry while dwelling in obscurity

5. both were rejected in their first attempt to deliver their kinsmen

6. both were examples of great humility despite their high calling

7. both performed great signs and wonders before Jews and Gentiles alike

8. both were ordained to be prophets of God, spiritual leaders, and shepherd rulers

9. both would institute a covenant between God and His people

10. both would save and lead a people of God made up of Jews and Gentiles united as one

11. both spoke to God face to face, and were like God to their brethren

12. both would die, but their bodies would not be found.

ALL: *"But now, you who were once far off have been brought near through the shedding of the Messiah's blood. For he himself is our shalom—he has made us both one and has broken down the middle wall which divided us."* **Ephesians 2:13–14 CJB**

DAYENU – "IT WOULD HAVE BEEN ENOUGH" (OPTIONAL)

(A traditional recitation, abridged. It can also be divided into "men" and "women" portions.)

ALL: *God has done many awesome deeds on our behalf; for all these and more we praise His Name and say, "Dayenu—it would have been enough!"*

ADULTS: *If God had merely rescued us from Egypt but not punished the Egyptians…*

CHILDREN: *Dayenu!*

ADULTS: *If God had merely destroyed their gods but not given us their property…*

CHILDREN: *Dayenu!*

ADULTS *If God had merely split the sea for us but not drowned our enemies…*

CHILDREN: *Dayenu!*

ADULTS: *If God had merely supplied us in the desert forty years but not fed us manna…*

CHILDREN: *Dayenu!*

ADULTS: If God had merely brought us to Mount Sinai but not given us the Torah...

CHILDREN: *Dayenu!*

ALL: *God has done all these things and more—He has made us His People...Dayenu!*

Worship Songs
"Dayenu" – Hebrew Song (Optional)

Verse 1

I-lu ho-tzi, ho-tzi-a-nu, ho-tzi-a-nu mi-mitz-ra-yim
Ho-tzi-a-nu, mi-mitz-ra-yim, da-ye-nu!
(Translation: Had God done nothing but save us from the land of Egypt, for that alone we would have been satisfied!)

Chorus

Dai-dai-ye-nu! (3x) Da-ye-nu (3x)
Dai-dai-ye-nu! (3x) Da-ye-nu! (2x)

Verse 2

I-lu na-tan na-tan la-nu, na-tan la-nu et ha-to-rah
Na-tan la-nu, et ha-to-rah, da-ye-nu!
(Translation: Had God given us nothing but the Torah, *for that alone we would have been satisfied)*
(Repeat Chorus)

"The Horse and Rider" – The Exodus Song (Optional)

I will sing unto the Lord for He has triumphed gloriously,

The horse and rider thrown into the se-ee-ea!

I will sing unto the Lord for He has triumphed gloriously,

The horse and rider thrown into the sea!

The Lord! My God! My strength! My song! Is now, become my vic-tor - y - y!

The Lord! My God! My strength! My song! Is now, become my victory!

The Lord is God and [clap] – I will praise Him, My Father is God and, I-I will ex-alt Him! The Lord is God and [clap] – I will praise Him, My Father is God and, I-I will exalt Him!

(Sing through 2x)

STEP 6

PASSOVER ELEMENTS

PASSOVER LAMB – "PESACH"

(The sacrificed lamb is represented on the Seder plate by a lamb shank bone.)

HOST: As read earlier in Exodus 12, on the tenth to the fourteenth day of the month of Aviv, the households would pick their lambs and examine them for defects. The blood seen upon their doors would spare their firstborn from death. Once the Temple was destroyed in AD 70, Jews could no longer offer the sacrifices prescribed in the Torah. Today the shank bone remains in remembrance of the sacrificed lambs. As Messianic believers, we see a clear typology in the Pesach lamb of Yeshua, who would be that final temple sacrifice for His firstborn (Israel). The prophets Isaiah and John speak of Him.

PERSON 2: *"Who would have believed our report? And to whom hath the arm of YHVH been revealed? For he shot up right forth as a sapling, And as a root out of a dry ground; He had no form* *nor comeliness, that we should look upon him, nor beauty that we should delight in him. Surely our diseases he did bear, and our pains he carried; whereas we did esteem him stricken, smitten of God, and afflicted. But he was wounded because of our transgressions, he was crushed because of our iniquities: the chastisement of our welfare was upon him, and with his stripes we were healed. All we like sheep did go astray, we turned every one to his own way; and YHVH hath made to light on him the iniquity of us all. He was oppressed, though he humbled himself and opened not his mouth; as a lamb that is led to the slaughter, and as a sheep that before her shearers is dumb; yea, he opened not his mouth."* **Isaiah 53:1–7 JPS**

ALL: *"The next day he saw Yeshua coming to him and said, "Behold, the Lamb of God who takes away the sin of the world!""*
John 1:29 NASB

HOST: Yeshua entered Jerusalem on the same day the paschal lambs were selected for examination, better known to the Church as Palm Sunday. If one calculated from the decree given to rebuild Jerusalem, until when "One Anointed" (meaning "Messiah") would enter Jerusalem in His role as prince (as prophesied in the book of Daniel), it would bring you to April 6, AD 32,[4] the historical last week of Yeshua's life! Rulers in the Ancient Near East rode horses when coming to conquer, and donkeys if they came in peace. It was on this very day that Yeshua was greeted as Messiah with shouts of "Hosanna!" meaning "to save."

---

4   See Section 3 Chapter 7 for more information in how this date is determined.

HOSTESS: "The next day, the large crowd that had come for the festival heard that Yeshua was on his way into Jerusalem. They took palm branches and went out to meet him, shouting, *'Deliver us!' 'Blessed is he who comes in the name of YHVH, the King of Isra'el!'* After finding a donkey colt, Yeshua mounted it, just as the Tanakh says - *'Daughter of Tziyon, don't be afraid! Look! your King is coming, sitting on a donkey's colt.'* "
John 12:12-15 CJB

READER: " *'Know therefore and discern, that from the going forth of the word to restore and to build Jerusalem unto one anointed, a prince, shall be seven weeks; and for threescore and two weeks it shall be built again, with broad place and moat, but in troublous times. And after the threescore and two weeks shall an anointed one be cut off.'* " **Daniel 9:25–26a JPS**

READER: *"Rejoice greatly, O daughter of Zion, shout, O daughter of Jerusalem; behold, thy king cometh unto thee, he is triumphant, and victorious, lowly, and riding upon an asss, even upon a colt the foal of an ass."* **Zechariah 9:9 JPS**

ROASTED EGG – "BEITZAH" OR "CHAGIGAH"

HOST: A roasted egg is universally found on the Seder plate. It is either called "beitzah" (egg), or "chagigah" (festival offering). The following are four rabbinic views on why it is included: 1) It represents a second festival sacrifice that was roasted and offered up on the three Pilgrimage Feasts (Passover, Shavuot, and Succoth); 2) It typifies giving God the day's "first fruits" since hens typically lay eggs in the morning; 3) As a symbol of mourning the destruction of the Second Temple in AD 70 ; and 4) Since eggs have no visible beginning or end, it represents the "cycle of life": birth, death, and rebirth.

HOSTESS: Perhaps it found its way into our Seder in the same way eggs are used to celebrate Resurrection Day (Easter); neither has a biblical nor historical reference to explain them. No blessing is said over this element, but it is often dipped in the salt water, and can be partaken of at any time. Finally, we come to the time when we will partake of that second cup of wine, the cup of deliverance, in gratitude for all God has done!

DRINKING THE SECOND CUP OF WINE

בָּרוּךְ אַתָּה יְהוָה אֱלֹהֵינוּ מֶלֶךְ הָעוֹלָם, בּוֹרֵא פְּרִי הַגָּפֶן. אָמֵן

HOST: *Baruch atah YHVH, Eloheinu Melech ha-olom, borey p'ri hagafen.* Amen.

ALL: Blessed are You, YHVH our God, King of the Universe, who creates the fruit of the vine. Amen.

(Lean left and partake of the second cup of wine.)

UNLEAVENED BREAD – "MATZAH"

(Host takes the piece of matzah left in the unity bag and holds it up. Table leaders should distribute the 1/4 pieces of matzah on their Seder plates so each person has one.)

HOST: This portion of the middle matzah still remaining in the unity bag represents the "bread of affliction" that our ancestors ate in haste that Passover night before they were driven out of Egypt. Rabbis have given different explanations for what these three matzot represent: 1) The Patriarchs: Abraham, Isaac, and Jacob—three generations, yet one family; 2) Three Types of Worshippers: Kohen, Levites, and other Israelites—each with distinct roles, yet one people before God; 3) Three Divisions of the Tanakh[5]: the *Torah* (Law), *Nevi'im* (Prophets), and *Ketuvim* (Writings)—three categories comprising the Holy Scriptures. As Messianic believers, we offer an alternative view; 4) The Tri-Unity (Triune) Godhead: Father, Son and Holy Spirit—three distinct entities with separate functions, yet all of the same Divine Nature being One Godhead.[6]

HOSTESS: The Rabbinic options offer no explanation for why the middle matzah is removed from the unity bag, nor the symbolism of matzah being striped, pierced, wrapped in white linen and hidden away for a period of time. Yet all of

---

5   The consonants from the the Torah, Nevi'im, and Ketuvim form the word "TaNaKh".

6   See Section 3 Chapter 8 for more information on the Trinune nature of the Godhead.

these things were true of the sinless life of Yeshua who suffered and died so that we could be "passed over" in judgment. As the "Middle Person" of the Triune Godhead, Yeshua was temporarily separated (broken away) from His abode to dwell "in flesh" among us, and to fulfill the task for which He came. His last words were: *"It is finished"* (John 19:30). He had paid the redemption price for humanity's guilt and justified the many before our righteous and Holy Father!

PERSON 3: *"By oppression and judgment he was taken away, and with his generation who did reason? For he was cut off out of the land of the living, for the transgression of my people to whom the stroke was due. And they made his grave with the wicked, and with the rich his tomb; although he had done no violence, neither was any deceit in his mouth. Yet it pleased YHVH to crush him by disease; to see if his soul would offer itself in restitution. That he might see his seed, prolong his days, And that the purpose of YHVH might prosper by his hand: Of the travail of his soul he shall see to the full, even My servant, who by his knowledge did justify the Righteous One to the many, and their iniquities he did bear."*
Isaiah 53:8–11 JPS

ALL: *"But He, having offered one sacrifice for sins for all time, SAT DOWN AT THE RIGHT HAND OF GOD, waiting from that time onward UNTIL HIS ENEMIES BE MADE A FOOTSTOOL FOR HIS FEET."* **Hebrews 10:12–13 NASB**

HOST: Let us take a piece of matzah as we say the blessing:

בָּרוּךְ אַתָּה יְהֹוָה אֱלֹהֵינוּ מֶלֶךְ הָעוֹלָם אֲשֶׁר קִדְּשָׁנוּ בְּמִצְוֹתָיו וְצִוָּנוּ עַל אֲכִילַת
מַצָּ. אָמֵן.

*Baruch atah YHVH, Eloheinu Melech ha-olom, Asher kidshanu
b'mitzvotav, v'tzi-vanu, al achilat matzah.* Amen.

ALL: Blessed are You, YHVH our God, King of the Universe,
who sanctified us with His commandments, commanding us
concerning the eating of unleavened bread. Amen.

(Everyone leans left and partakes of the matzah.)

BITTER HERBS – "MAROR"

*(Host holds up the horseradish root, while table leaders pass the
prepared horseradish around. Everyone should take enough to put
on two separate servings of matzah.)*

HOST: On all other nights we eat all kinds of vegetables, but
tonight we eat only maror. We allow it to bring tears to our eyes
in remembrance of our ancestors' 400 years of bondage. This
time we do not lean left, as slaves would "eat upright and in
haste" like our ancestors did that night.

ALL: *"And they made their lives bitter with hard service, in mortar and in brick, and in all manner of service in the field; in all their service, wherein they made them serve with rigour."*
Exodus 1:14 JPS

בָּרוּךְ אַתָּה יְהוָה אֱלֹהֵינוּ מֶלֶךְ הָעוֹלָם אֲשֶׁר קִדְּשָׁנוּ בְּמִצְוֹתָיו וְצִוָּנוּ עַל אֲכִילַת
מָרוֹר. אָמֵן

HOST: *Baruch atah YHVH Eloheinu Melech ha-olom, Asher kidshanu B'mitzvotav, v'tzi-vanu al achilat maror.* Amen.

ALL: Blessed are You, YHVH our God, Ruler of the universe, who set us apart by His work, and commanded us to eat bitter herbs. Amen.

(Everyone sit up straight to partake of the matzah and herbs.)

HILLEL SANDWICH: MAROR AND CHAROSET – "KORESH"

(Table leaders pass the charoset. Everyone puts both the maror and charoset on this piece of matzah.)

HOST: Having already dipped the parsley into salt water, we now dip the bitter maror into the sweet charoset. Charoset is meant to represent the mortar used to make bricks, but also to be a reminder that bitter circumstances can be sweetened by hope! The Israelites had hope that God saw their pain and would answer their prayers. At Yeshua's last Passover He seems to have carried out this tradition—or perhaps even instituted it! Yeshua gave honor to Judas when He allowed him to dip first. It was a sweet offer of hope and warning of what he was doing, while affording him the opportunity to repent.

READER: "As they were reclining and eating, Yeshua said, *'Yes! I tell you that one of you is going to betray me... it's one of the Twelve,'* he said to them, *'someone dipping matzah in the dish with me.'* " **Mark 14:18, 20 CJB**

HOSTESS: From generation to generation, God has consistently given us warnings and opportunities to repent and avoid the consequences of our sins. Even as Adam was warned, so was Cain.

READER: "And YHVH said unto Cain: *'Why art thou wroth? and why is thy countenance fallen? If thou doest well, shall it not be lifted up? And if thou doest not well, sin coucheth at the door; and unto thee is its desire, but thou mayest rule over it.'* " **Genesis 4:6–7 JPS**

HOST: Take and eat. This concludes the first portion of our Seder. Haggadot should be set aside to avoid spills and to continue our Seder after the meal.

STEP 7

PASSOVER MEAL —
"SHULCHAN AROCH"

(At this time, the main meal is served. You may also choose to have a time of worship before and/or after the meal is served.)

STEP 8

RETURN TO THE SEDER

EATING OF THE AFIKOMEN – "TSAPHUN"

(Host assures the Afikomen was found, brings up the child who found it, and prepares to buy it back from the child, usually $1–$5)

HOST: It is time to return to our Seder and partake of the final food of the night—the *Afikomen*, which was found by this person here. I am going to redeem it with money.

(Pause to give money)

This *Afikomen* which I redeemed is to be shared by everyone in the room who partook of the Passover meal. We will not eat it until everyone has gotten a piece. I will unwrap it from the linen cloth I hid it in, break off a small piece for myself, and pass it around the table for each to do likewise. Once everyone has a piece, we will say the blessing and partake of it. As it is being passed, we would like to share another view of the origins of the *Afikomen* other than as dessert, as Rabbinic tradition claims. I'm sure after partaking of matzah, it's unlikely anyone would choose it as a dessert.

(If there is more than one table, the last person passes it to the next table.)

HOSTESS: Up until the destruction of the Temple in AD 70, both rabbinic Jews and those who followed Yeshua's teachings still celebrated these Appointed Seasons together. Perhaps some of their traditions blended. We are reminded that *"Afikomen"* means "to come" and was instituted in this era when Greek was the common language. We also know from the B'rit Hadashah (New Covenant) that Yeshua instituted an ordinance much like this at His Last Supper. After the meal, He took a piece of unleavened bread, broke it, and shared it with everyone at the Passover table. He used the matzah as a symbol of His being like the unblemished Pesach lambs whose lifeblood caused death to "pass over" their ancestors' homes in Egypt that night. He was not suggesting it was His actual body, for He was still alive; rather it was to be a remembrance of His imminent sacrificial death until He comes again.

READER: *"Yeshua said to them, "I am the bread of life; he who comes to Me will not hunger, and he who believes in Me will never thirst.""* **John 6:35 NASB**

READER: *"Also, taking a piece of matzah, he made the blessing, broke it, gave it to them and said, 'This is my body, which is being given for you; do this in memory of me.'"* **Luke 22:19 CJB**

HOST: Whether or not Yeshua instituted this practice, or these elements were instituted into the Passover Seders at practically the same times, rabbis say it is incumbent upon us to partake of this *Afikomen* as the pinnacle element of the Seder.

בָּרוּךְ אַתָּה יְהוָה אֱלֹהֵינוּ מֶלֶךְ הָעוֹלָם, הַמּוֹצִיא לֶחֶם מִן הָאָרֶץ. אָמֵן

Baruch atah YHVH Eloheinu Melech ha-olom ha-motzi lechem min ha-aretz. Amen.

ALL: Blessed are You, YHVH our God, King of the Universe, who brings forth bread from the earth. Amen.

(Lean left and partake of the Afikomen.)

THIRD CUP OF WINE: REDEMPTION – "HA GEULAH BORAYCH"

(Make sure wine has been poured to partake of the third cup.)

ALL: *"I will also redeem you with an outstretched arm and great judgements."* **Exodus 6:6c JPS**

HOST: This third glass of wine celebrates the redemption of God's people from bondage. Death struck the firstborn in every household not covered by the blood of a spotless lamb—from their animals to the appointed heir to Pharaoh's throne—finally convincing Pharaoh to let YHVH's people go! They left with their belongings as well as gifts from awestruck Egyptians, and those Gentile families who also placed blood upon their doorways. We also see this tradition at the Last Seder Yeshua celebrated. After the meal, then breaking the bread He had shared with His disciples, He took a cup of wine and spoke of it symbolically as His blood. It represented the blood He would soon offer in atonement for their sins. It would also inaugurate a "New Covenant," as foretold by the prophet Jeremiah. Together, these two Seder elements He instituted at His Last Supper have become known to the Church as "Communion."

PERSON 2: *"He did the same with the cup after the meal, saying, 'This cup is the New Covenant, ratified by my blood, which is being poured out for you.'"* **Luke 22:19–20 CJB**

PERSON 3: *"Behold, the days come,* saith YHVH, *that I will make a new covenant with the house of Israel, and with the house of Judah; not according to the covenant that I made with their fathers in the day that I took them by the hand to bring them out of the land of Egypt; forasmuch as they broke My covenant, although I was a lord over them,* saith YHVH. *But this is the covenant that I will make with the house of Israel after those days,* saith YHVH. *I will put My law in their inward parts, and in their heart will I write it; and I will be their God, and they shall be My people."* **Jeremiah 31:31–33 JPS**

HOST: Let us raise our cups again as we lean left and say: *Baruch atah YHVH Eloheinu Melech ha-olom, Borey p'ri hagafen.* Amen.

בָּרוּךְ אַתָּה יְהוָה אֱלֹהֵינוּ מֶלֶךְ הָעוֹלָם, בּוֹרֵא פְּרִי הַגָּפֶן. אָמֵן

ALL: Blessed are You, YHVH our God, King of the Universe, who creates the fruit of the vine. Amen.

(Lean left and drink of the third cup.)

«ELIJAH THE PROPHET – "ELIYAHU HANAVI"

(The host lifts up Elijah's cup from the empty place setting at his left.)

ALL: *"Behold, I will send you Elijah the prophet Before the coming of the great and terrible day of YHVH."* **Malachi 4:23 JPS**

HOST: One of the last Seder traditions is meant to encourage our hope that the Davidic King is soon to come. Our ancestors believed He would judge the nations, then establish a Kingdom of Righteousness in Jerusalem. The main difference between Rabbinic and Messianic thought is whether there are two Messiahs (one who will suffer like Joseph, and one who will reign like David); or two comings of one Messiah (the first time suffering rejection like Joseph, the second time to be received and reign like David). Scripture also speaks of Elijah the prophet, whom God took up to Heaven without experiencing death, returning to prepare Israel for this coming Messiah. Historically, it has been Israel's hope that Elijah will return at Passover, so it is the custom that we set a place for him at our table. It is also part of our tradition to ask one of the children to volunteer to go to the door and see if Elijah has come this year.

(The host asks for a child to volunteer and open the door, look and report if Elijah was found.)

HOST: He has not come this year, but we sing the following song as a hope and prayer that he will come soon, and usher in the reign of the Messianic Son of David in our lifetime!

"ELIYAHU HANAVI" – ELIJAH THE PROPHET SONG (OPTIONAL)

(Can be sung in Hebrew, or recited in English if the song is not known.)

1st Portion	*Eliyahu ha'na-vi*	*Elijah the prophet*
	Eliyahu ha'tish-bi	*Elijah the Tishbite*
	Eliyahu, Eliyahu	*Elijah, Elijah*
	Eliya-ah-hu ha'gila-di	*Elijah the Giladite*

2nd Portion	*Bim he'rah v'ya mei-nu*	*May he come quickly*
	Ya-a-vo, elei-ei-nu	*In our days*
	Im Mashiach, ben Da-vid	*With the Messiah, the Son of David*
	Im Mashiach, ben Da-vid	*With the Messiah, the Son of David*

(Repeat first portion to end song.)

HOSTESS: The B'rit Hadashah (New Covenant) speaks of two witnesses who come to earth in the last days before the Messiah. Both will do miracles identical to, and only done by, Elijah or Moses. These are also the only two prophets associated with the Passover events, although as mentioned before, Moses is rarely included by name in traditional Haggadot despite being the main character in the Exodus account. Elijah was not yet born in the days of the Exodus, yet they both appear to have an end-times mission in ushering in the Messiah.

PERSON 1: *"And I will grant authority to my two witnesses, and they will prophesy for twelve hundred and sixty days, clothed in sackcloth… These have the power to shut up the sky, so that rain will not fall during the days of their prophesying [like Elijah]; and they have power over the waters to turn them into blood, and to strike the earth with every plague, as often as they desire [like Moses]."* **Revelation 11:3, 6 NASB**

FOURTH CUP OF WINE: PRAISE – "HALLEL"

(Wine cups should be filled for the fourth and final time.)

ALL: *"I will take you as my own people and I will be your God."* **Exodus 6:7 JPS**

HOST: This is the cup of Hallel, meaning "praise." The word hallelujah in Hebrew is *HalleluYah*, meaning "Praise Yah," the poetic abbreviation for YHVH's name. These passages represent the joy of being God's people of faith. Scripture tells us that faith is "assurance of things hoped for, not seen" (Hebrews 11:6). We are told all God's people will live by faith, not yet seeing the promises hoped for by us or our ancestors. As Messianic Jews, we anticipate a resurrection of the body, soul, and spirit of all who have trusted in His provision of atonement and eternal life. Freed from sin and its curse, we will dwell with Him on Earth when He returns—to establish a Righteous Kingdom!

ALL: *"And I will walk among you, and will be your God, and ye shall be My people."* **Leviticus 26:12 JPS**

PERSON 2: *"And ye shall know that I am YHVH, when I have opened your graves, and caused you to come up out of your graves, O My people. And I will put My Spirit in you, and ye shall live, and I will place you in your own land; and ye shall know that I YHVH have spoken, and performed it,'* saith YHVH.*"*
Ezekiel 37:13–14 JPS

PERSON 3: *"'Truly it is I that have established My king upon Zion, My holy mountain.'* I will tell of the decree: YHVH said unto me: *'Thou art My son, this day have I begotten thee. Ask of Me, and I will give the nations for thine inheritance, and the ends of the earth for thy possession."* **Psalm 2:6-8 JPS**

HOST: Let us pray: *Baruch atah YHVH, Eloheinu Melech ha-olom, Borey p'ri hagafen.* Amen.

ALL: Blessed are You, YHVH our God, King of the Universe, who creates the fruit of the vine. Amen.

בָּרוּךְ אַתָּה יְהֹוָה אֱלֹהֵינוּ מֶלֶךְ הָעוֹלָם, בּוֹרֵא פְּרִי הַגָּפֶן. אָמֵן

(All lean left for the last time, as we drink the fourth cup of wine.)

FULFILLMENT OF THE SPRING APPOINTED FEASTS

HOST: As followers of Messiah, we believe these Appointed Seasons of YHVH are actually "appointments with us" at His first and second Comings! The Spring Feasts were fulfilled:

- **Passover** – as the Lamb of God who hung on a stake, and took His last breath at the hour the Pesach lambs were being slaughtered in Jerusalem
- **Unleavened Bread** – He was examined for sin from the day the Pesach lambs were inspected until the eighth day when He was risen as a witness that He was without sin
- **Firstfruits** – His resurrection concurred with the morning the High Priest would wave a sheaf of the firstfruits of new grain before YHVH to be accepted by Him.

PERSON 1: "And YHVH spoke unto Moses, saying: *Speak unto the children of Israel, and say unto them: When ye are come into the land which I give unto you, and shall reap the harvest thereof, then ye shall bring the sheaf of the first-fruits of your harvest unto the priest. And he shall wave the sheaf before YHVH, to be accepted for you; on the morrow after the sabbath the priest shall wave it.*"
Leviticus 23:9–11 JPS

PERSON 2: *"If it is only for this life that we have put our hope in the Messiah, we are more pitiable than anyone. But the fact is that the Messiah has been raised from the dead, the firstfruits of those* *who have died.".... "But each in his own order: the Messiah is the firstfruits; then those who belong to the Messiah, at the time of his coming; then the culmination, when he hands over the Kingdom to God the Father, after having put an end to every rulership, yes, to every authority and power."* **1 Corinthians 15:19–20, 23–24 CJB**

HOSTESS: The Feast of Firstfruits was fulfilled on Resurrection Sunday. On this appointed date God met with just one person, the High Priest. He was to represent the nation before God, and as their spiritual leader make intercession for them. In AD 32, the year Messiah died:

- **Passover** (14th of Aviv): fell on the sixth day of the week (Good Friday), when at 3 p.m. he took his last breath and was laid in a tomb (first day of His death).
- **First Day of Unleavened Bread** (15th of Aviv): fell on the weekly Sabbath, which begins at sundown (second day of His death).
- **Firstfruits** (not an ordinal date on the calendar): always falls on the day after the weekly Sabbath of the Passover Season (Sunday and third day of His death).[7]

In AD 32, Firstfruits followed a "double Sabbath" (weekly and first day of Unleavened Bread). Just as He foretold His disciples, Yeshua arose from the grave on the third day-- better known to the world as Easter Sunday. He now sits at the Father's right hand as our King and High Priest in the order of Melchizedek![8]

---

7 See Section 3 Chapter 9 for more information on Yeshua's death and resurrection as prophetic fulfillments.

8 See Section 3 Chapter 10 for more information on Melchizedek.

PERSON 3: "A Psalm of David. YHVH saith unto my lord (Adonai): *'Sit thou at My right hand, until I make thine enemies thy footstool.'* ... "YHVH hath sworn, and will not repent: *'Thou art a priest for ever after the manner of Melchizedek.'* The lord at thy right hand doth crush kings in the day of His wrath."
Psalm 110:1, 4–5 JPS

READING OF PSALMS

HOST: It was customary for worshippers to ascend the Temple Mount after the Passover singing the psalms of praise. Let us close with some excerpts from the psalms read responsively.

PSALM 117 JPS

ALL: *"O praise YHVH, all ye nations; laud Him, all ye peoples; For His mercy is great toward us; and the truth of YHVH endureth forever. HalleluYah."*

PSALM 118:14–29 JPS

MEN: *"YHVH is my strength and song; and He is become my salvation."*

WOMEN: *"The voice of rejoicing and salvation is in the tents of the righteous; the right hand of YHVH doeth valiantly."*

MEN: *"The right hand of YHVH is exalted; The right hand of YHVH doeth valiantly."*

WOMEN: *"I shall not die, but live, and declare the works of YHVH."*

MEN: *"YHVH hath chastened me sore; but He hath not given me over unto death."*

WOMEN: *"Open to me the gates of righteousness; I will enter into them, I will give thanks unto YHVH."*

MEN: *"This is the gate of YHVH. The righteous shall enter into it."*

WOMEN: *"I will give thanks unto Thee, for Thou hast answered me, and art become my salvation."*

MEN: *"The stone which the builders rejected is become the chief cornerstone."*

WOMEN: *"This is YHVH's doing; it is marvelous in our eyes."*

MEN: *"This is the day which YHVH hath made; we will rejoice and be glad in it."*

WOMEN: *"We beseech Thee, O YHVH, save now! We beseech Thee, O YHVH, make us now to prosper!"*

MEN: *"Blessed be he that cometh in the name of YHVH; we bless you out of the house of YHVH."*

WOMEN: *"YHVH is God, and hath given us light; order the festival procession with boughs, even unto the horns of the altar."*

ALL: *"Thou art my God, and I will give thanks unto Thee; Thou art my God, I will exalt Thee. O give thanks unto YHVH, for He is good, for His mercy endureth for ever."*

PSALM 136:1–4, 10–15, 26 JPS

ALL: *"O give thanks unto YHVH, for he is good, for His mercy endureth forever. O give thanks unto the God of gods, for His mercy endureth forever. O give thanks unto the Lord of lords, for His mercy endureth forever. To Him who alone doeth great wonders, for His mercy endureth forever."*

MEN	WOMEN
"To Him that smote Egypt in their first-born,	*for His mercy endureth forever.*
And brought out Israel from among them,	*for His mercy endureth forever.*
A strong hand, and with an outstretched arm,	*for His mercy endureth forever."*
"To Him who divided the Red Sea in sunder,	*for His mercy endureth forever.*
And made Israel to pass through the midst of it,	*for His mercy endureth forever.*
But overthrew Pharaoh and his host in the Red Sea,	*for His mercy endureth forever.*
To Him that led His people through the wilderness,	*for His mercy endureth forever."*

ALL: *"O give thanks unto the God of heaven, for His mercy endureth forever."*

HOST: Our Seder is now complete. Our hope and prayer is that next year we might celebrate the Passover together in Jerusalem with the King of Kings!

ALL: We say: *"La' Shanah Haba'ah Bi' Yerushalayim,"* or *"Next Year in Jerusalem!"*

לְשָׁנָה הַבָּאה בִּירוּנָשָׁלִים

"LA SHANAH HABA 'AH BI YERUSHALAYIM" – SONG (OPTIONAL)

*(The above can be recited or sung. If sung, each time
it is repeated it speeds up.)*

---

3 A DEEPER STUDY OF THE SEDER

6

YHVH: THE PERSONAL NAME OF GOD

The personal name of God is represented by the Tetragrammaton, meaning "four letters" in Greek. It is made up of these four Hebrew consonants: יהוה (YHVH). Without vowels, it's pronounced Yahveh or Yahweh. Vowels were not included in most ancient Jewish writings, but the vowels E-O-A were consistently found in recently discovered ancient manuscripts, rendering the pronunciation "Yehovah."[9]

God's personal name is first introduced in Genesis 2, when the Creation account moves from an overview of God's creative work as Elohim in Genesis 1 to describing a more intimate God who intended to personally engage with His Creation. Introducing Himself into "His-Story" as YHVH Elohim, God is expressing His love and desire for a personal relationship. Scripture describes the idea of intimacy as "knowing" (ידע yada),

---

9   Some examples of where these 3 vowels are found with the Tetragrammaton include: Aleppo Codex, Leningrad Codex, Nash Papyrus, and among the Dead Sea Scrolls. There have been over 1000 findings: https://www.nehemiaswall.com/YHVH-manuscripts

meaning: "experience, have relations with." This same word is used to express the intimacy and trust between a husband and wife.

We also see this yearning in His Covenant relationships with Israel in the *Tenach* (Old Testament) and the Church in the New Testament. His personal name is used by Eve (Genesis 4:1); Enosh (Genesis 4:26); Noah (Genesis 9:26); Abraham and Sarah (Genesis 12:8, 16:2, 24:12); Isaac and Rebekah (Genesis 25:21, 23); Jacob, Leah, and Rachel (Genesis 28:16, 29:31, 30:24); and even some who sought other gods (Genesis 30:27; 39:2). Calling on "the Name of YHVH" was lost to the children of Israel by the fourth generation. The narrative assures us that YHVH is with Joseph in Egypt, but neither Joseph nor any of his eleven brothers ever calls on YHVH by name. In Genesis 49:18, following a disturbing prophetic word Jacob proclaims over his son Dan, Jacob cries out: "For Your salvation I wait, O YHVH."

This explains why God personally introduces Himself to Moses in Exodus 3:15 as "YHVH, the God of your fathers, the God of Abraham, the God of Isaac, and the God of Jacob." YHVH is to be God's "memorial name to all generations." Moses is ordered to restore its use among the Israelites. It is in this name that Moses is given the Ten Commandments (Exodus 20), and Aaron and the future Levitical high priests are told to bless the Israelites (Numbers 6:24–27).

In English versions of both the Jewish Scriptures and most Christian Bibles, LORD (all caps), is substituted for God's name. Religious tradition commonly gives the following reasons for not using God's personal name:

1. it is too sacred to be used

2. fear of pronouncing it wrong, which would be a sin

3. as a sign of respect

All these reasons seem to disregard God's higher mandate to call on the name of YHVH in favor of established traditions. His personal name is used over 6,800 times in Scripture! The second most commonly used reference to Israel's God is the title אונ' (Adonai), meaning "Lord, Master," which is used around 2,500 times, but can also refer to a king, father, husband, prophet, boss, etc.

Elohim אלה'ם is simply the plural form of "god" or "el" (אל). In Scripture it is not only used for Israel's God, but the pagan gods. Yeshua (Jesus) is the personal name of the second member of the Godhead, but He also has many titles: Messiah (Christ), Adonai (Lord), Immanuel (God with us), and more. There is no title used for Israel's God that has not been assumed by other gods—YHVH, or Yehovah with the vowels, is the *only* name by which no other god has been called!

7

THE COMING OF MESSIAH
PROPHESIED IN DANIEL 9

Daniel 9 has the only prophetic text in the entire Jewish Scriptures that definitively addresses the exact time of Messiah's coming:

> *"Seventy weeks are decreed upon thy people and upon thy holy city, to finish the transgression, and to make an end of sin, and to forgive iniquity, and to bring in everlasting righteousness, and to seal vision and prophet, and to anoint the most holy place. Know therefore and discern, that from the going forth of the word to restore and to build Jerusalem unto one anointed, a prince, shall be seven weeks; and for threescore and two weeks, it shall be built again, with broad place and moat, but in troublous times. And after the threescore and two weeks shall an anointed one, be cut off, and be no more; and the people of a prince that shall come shall destroy the city and the sanctuary; but his end shall be with a flood; and unto the end of the war desolations are determined."* **Daniel 9:24–26 JPS**

To unravel this mystery that reveals the timing of this coming anointed prince, meaning Messiah, we need to look at the phrases highlighted in the verses above, as well as some information surrounding this prophecy.

1. Seventy weeks – To figure out the timing of this coming one requires an understanding of how biblical Hebrew numbers were counted. The Hebrew reads: "שבע'ם שבע'ם" (seventy sevens). The word for seven, " שבוע" (sheva), can mean a period of seven days (Feast of Weeks), or years (weeks of years, as in seventy years of Israel's captivity in Babylon). Daniel understood this, as we see in the Scripture below:

> *"In the first year of Darius the son of Ahasuerus, of the seed of the Medes, who was made king over the realm of the Chaldeans; in the first year of his reign I, Daniel meditated in the books, over the number of the years, whereof the word of YHVH came to Jeremiah the prophet, that He would accomplish for the desolations of Jerusalem seventy years."* **Daniel 9:1–2 JPS**

> "For thus saith YHVH: '*After seventy years are accomplished for Babylon, I will remember you, and perform My good word toward you, in causing you to return to this place.*' "
> **Jeremiah 29:10 JPS**

Daniel also knew that Israel's captivity in Babylon for seventy years was not a random decision, but based on the seventy weeks of years (or 490 years) that Israel had been sinning against God by not giving their land a Sabbath rest. That time was nearing an end, and Daniel was acknowledging that God's judgment was justly deserved, in accordance with breaking Mosaic Law:

> "And YHVH spoke unto Moses in mount Sinai, saying, *'Speak unto the children of Israel, and say unto them, When ye come into the land which I give you, then shall the land keep a sabbath unto YHVH. Six years thou shalt sow thy field, and six years thou shalt prune thy vineyard, and gather in the produce thereof. But in* **the seventh year shall be a sabbath of solemn rest for the land,** *a sabbath unto YHVH: thou shalt neither sow thy field, nor prune thy vineyard."*
> **Leviticus 25:1–4 JPS** (emphasis added)

They remained captive for all the years they should have rested the land during their 490 years of living in Israel (seventy years of seven). Therefore, it would make perfect sense that this prophecy of seventy weeks in Daniel 9 is referring to another seventy weeks of years (490 years) in which God gives them back the land, and will wait to see if they will obey and receive their anointed prince when He comes.

2. "Know therefore and discern" – This is the only prophecy in Tanakh that is prefaced with an exhortation that stresses its importance. It is given in the imperative form that makes it a command, not a suggestion. The word to know,'עד , as spoken of in Chapter 1, is commanding His people to be acquainted with the time of this prophecy's fulfillment. The word *sekhal* (שכל) or to discern, would mean to be prudent, ponder, gain insight. Yet very few Jews or Christians are even familiar with this prophecy, much less how to deduce the dating. *The Coming Prince* by Sir Robert Anderson and *Daniel's Prophecy of the 70 Weeks* by Alva J. McClain explain how one can calculate the exact date when Messiah entered Jerusalem before being put to death.

Rabbinic scholars remain unfamiliar with, or avoid deducing, the timing of this prophecy's fulfillment. The Babylonian Talmud (*Tractate Sanhedrin 97B*), written by rabbis in the fifth century AD, actually forbids anyone even attempting to calculate Messiah's coming under penalty of a curse! The Talmud is the source from which rabbinic Judaism determines Jewish laws and obedience for today. To further avoid "knowing and discerning" Messiah's arrival, back in the tenth century AD the book of Daniel was demoted from its previous position among the Prophets (Isaiah, Jeremiah, Ezekiel, etc.), to the back of the Tanakh among the Writings (Psalms, Proverbs, Job, etc.) This also precludes Daniel ever being read in the synagogues as a *Haftorah* portion (weekly Sabbath reading from the Prophets) that accompanies a weekly designated portion from the Torah (Moses's writings).

3. "From the going forth of the word to restore and to build Jerusalem" – The starting point for the countdown concerning this prophecy came after Daniel's lifetime. Gabriel gave Daniel the prophecy in 538 BC, the first year of King Darius's reign. While both Cyrus and Darius gave Ezra permission to rebuild the Temple, only Artaxerxes gave Nehemiah permission to return and rebuild the city of Jerusalem and its walls. This occurred in 445 BC, the twentieth year of Artaxerxes's reign:

1a "And it came to pass in the month Nisan, in the twentieth year of Artaxerxes the king"... 5 "And I said unto the king: *'If it please the king, and if thy servant have found favour in thy sight, that thou wouldest send me unto Judah, unto the city of my fathers' sepulchres, that I may build it*"... 7–8 "Moreover I said unto the king: *'If it please the king, let letters be given me to the governors beyond the River, that they may let me pass through till I come unto Judah; and a letter unto Asaph the keeper of the king's park, that he may give me timber to make beams for the gates of the castle which appertaineth to the house, and for the wall of the city, and for the house that I shall enter into.'* And the king granted me, according to the good hand of my God upon me." **Nehemiah 2:1a, 5, 7–8 JPS**

4. "One anointed, a prince" – The Hebrew word for anointed (מש'ח) is *Mashiach* or Messiah. (Mashiach translated to Greek is *Christos*, which then translated to English is Christ). Prince in this context is the word *nagid* (נג'ד) and also means "ruler, leader, one with authority." This anointed prince will "finish the transgression" (against the Mosaic Law); "make an end of sin" (through atonement); forgive iniquity (which only God can do); "bring in everlasting righteousness" (as a righteous king on the throne); "to seal vision and prophecy" (by fulfilling them all); and "anoint the most holy place" (entering the Holy of Holies as both priest and king) upon His return. There is no other "Anointed One" who qualifies and can accomplish these things but Messiah! This prophecy was given to Daniel so that those alive in the generation of its fulfillment, and those living afterward, could know for sure the "coming one" had fulfilled this prophetic timeline.

Daniel was in deep prayer when the angel Gabriel came to him this second time to give him this prophecy. Daniel implored God to forgive His people and rebuild Jerusalem, as well as the Sanctuary. Daniel was told that before God he was highly esteemed, which would make the message vitally important. The prophecy answered Daniel's prayerful appeal, but sadly informed him that his people would again rebel, resulting in a future destruction of both Temple and city. But Gabriel encouraged him with a greater hope: exact information to discern when the Messiah would come! That too would have a bittersweet outcome, for most of Israel would reject their Messianic Prince. Yet in the closing portion of Daniel's writings, God's faithful servant was assured that he, and all who are faithful to YHVH, would be resurrected to inherit an everlasting portion in Messiah's future kingdom.

"And many of them that sleep in the dust of the earth shall awake, some to everlasting life, and some to reproaches and everlasting abhorrence… But go thou thy way till the end be; and thou shalt rest, and shalt stand up to thy lot, at the end of the days." **Daniel 12:2, 13 JPS**

5. "Seven weeks; and for threescore and two weeks" – In verse 25, the prophesied seventy sevens (490 years) is broken up into two specific groupings and leaves a future one-week period (seven years) that will be fulfilled after an unknown time of delay, because this anointed one is cut off. The first seven weeks of seven years (or forty-nine years), marks the time it will take to rebuild Jerusalem and its walls, from the giving of the decree

(Nehemiah 2). Threescore and two weeks (sixty-two weeks of seven years equals 434 more years) will follow the rebuilding of Jerusalem until the Coming Prince arrives.

There is no chronological gap indicated between the first cluster of forty-nine years and the second cluster of 434 years. The separation merely indicates the number of years it took to rebuild the walls and city, versus the following number of years till Messiah's arrival (49 + 434 = 483 years). This leaves one future seven-year period for the completion of Daniel's seventy-year prophecy. At that time all that this "Anointed One" was prophesied to accomplish (His rightful, righteous reign) will come to fruition!

To properly calculate the exact date He will arrive requires breaking the biblical years into days. Scripture recorded the time in a year as being twelve months of thirty days, or 360 days. This can be calculated by looking at the record of days in the flood account (Genesis 7–8) and end-time prophecy (Revelation 11).

> "And God said: *'Let there be lights in the firmament of the heaven to divide the day from the night; and let them be for signs, and for seasons, and for days and years;*"
> **Genesis 1:14 JPS**

> "*In the six hundredth year of Noah's life, in the second month, on the seventeenth day of the month, on the same day were all the fountains of the great deep broken up, and the windows of heaven were opened.*" **Genesis 7:11 JPS**

"And the waters prevailed upon the earth a hundred and fifty days." **Genesis 7:24 JPS**

"And the waters returned from off the earth continually; and after the end of a hundred and fifty days the waters decreased. And the ark rested in the seventh month, on the seventeenth day of the month upon the mountains of Ararat."
Genesis 8:3–4 JPS

"…and they will tread underfoot the holy city for forty-two months. And I will grant authority to my two witnesses, and they will prophesy for twelve hundred and sixty days, clothed in sackcloth." **Revelation 11:2b–3 NASB**

The flood prevailed upon the earth for 150 days, starting on the seventeenth of the second month and ending on the seventeenth of the seventh month. Therefore, we know it prevailed for five full months, of thirty days = 150 days. Revelation has an end-time prophecy about Jerusalem again being "tread under" for forty-two months, while the "two witnesses" prophesy for the same amount of time: 42 months x 30 days = 1,260 days.

Sir Robert Anderson   calculates the exact dating by multiplying 360 days by 483 years, totaling 173,880 days from the decree to rebuild Jerusalem until the Messiah would arrive.[10] Artaxerxes started his reign in 465 BC. Nehemiah 2:1

---

10   These calculations are also aided by the Blue Letter Bible commentary notes of David Guzick, and notes of a dear colleague, James T Burr.

tells us the decree to rebuild the city was pronounced during his twentieth year, "in the month of Nisan." When no ordinal date was mentioned, Jewish custom understood it to be the first of the month. The first of Nisan on the Gregorian calendar would correlate to March 14, 445 BC. Yeshua began His ministry at thirty, in the fifteenth year of Tiberius, whose reign began in AD 14. Therefore, His ministry had to begin in AD 29.

"Now in the fifteenth year of the reign of Tiberius Caesar… in the high priesthood of Annas and Caiaphas, the word of God came to John, the son of Zacharias, in the wilderness. And he came into all the district around the Jordan, preaching a baptism of repentance for the forgiveness of sins"
Luke 3:1a, 2–3 NASB

"Now when all the people were baptized, Yeshua was also baptized, and while He was praying, heaven was opened, and the Holy Spirit descended upon Him in bodily form like a dove, and a voice came out of heaven, 'You are My beloved Son, in You I am well-pleased.' When He began His ministry, Yeshua Himself was about thirty years of age…"
Luke 3:21–23a NASB

It was three and a half years later in the days leading up to Passover that Yeshua entered Jerusalem on a donkey. With the aid of lunar charts, the exact dating of the ancient Passover holy days can be assessed. If we calculate 173,880 days from the decree to rebuild Jerusalem, it would bring Him into Jerusalem on April 6, AD 32. This is the very day most biblical historians believe Messiah entered Jerusalem on a donkey, as Ancient Near East kings did when they were coming in peace. He was hailed as the long-anticipated Son of David (Matthew 21:1–17).[11] It was on this day, now celebrated as Palm Sunday, Yeshua first allowed the people to publicly worship and acknowledged Him as their Messiah and Savior. It now makes sense why earlier in His ministry Yeshua refused to allow people to acknowledge Him as Messiah, for His time of arrival had not yet come!

> *"And the disciples went and did just as Yeshua had instructed them, and brought the donkey and the colt, and laid their coats on them; and he sat on the coasts."… "The crowds going ahead of Him, and those who followed, were shouting, 'Hosanna to the Son of David: BLESSED IS HE WHO COMES IN THE NAME OF YHVH ; Hosanna in the highest!"*
> **Matthew 21:6–7, 9 NASB (quoting Psalm 118:25)**

Summarized Calculation:

The dating below has been computed according to the Gregorian solar calendar, which has been in use by the western world since AD 1582.

- Artaxerxes's command on the first of Nissan computes to March 14, 445 BC
- 483 years of 360 days computes to April 6, AD 32 (by solar dating)
- 445 BC to AD 32 equals 476 years (1 BC to AD 1 is one year as there is no "0" year)

---

11   Other Scripture references concerning this event were read during the Seder: Isaiah 9:5-6, Zechariah 9:9, Psalm 118:24-26, and John 12:12-15.

- 476 years multiplied by 365 days computes into the solar calendar as 173,740 days
- Adding the recorded leap years in this time period adds 116 days, which brings the total to 173,856 days
- The 173,856 days from the decree to rebuild would come to March 14, AD 32, but still remains twenty-four days short of Daniel's prophecy of 173,880 days
- March 14 plus twenty-four days brings us to April 6, AD 32, accounting for all the 173,880 days from the decree by Artaxerxes to rebuild till the Messiah would arrive on the scene in Jerusalem riding on the donkey!

6. "Be cut off, and be no more" – This portion of the text extends past our study in regards to Messiah's first Advent. However, what should be noted is that this anointed one would be cut off (put to death) without establishing His Kingdom rather than accepted by Israel. The fact that the ruling aspect of His ministry has yet to be fulfilled does not negate that Yeshua was this prophesied prince, but rather that there has been an interruption between those sixty-nine weeks of years, and the seventieth week of Daniel is still to come!

7. "The people of a prince that shall come" – The Messiah would have had to come before the Temple was again destroyed, along with the city in AD 70 by Rome. Wars and devastations in the world at large have continued. When this unspecified time period comes to an end (sometimes referred to as the "Church Age" or "Mystery Age"), the final week (seven years) of Daniel's prophecy will be fulfilled. At that time the ministry of Messiah aforementioned in Daniel 9:24 will be completely fulfilled!

It seems a travesty that the people whom God originally instructed and revealed this prophecy to are not only ignorant of it, but superstitiously fearful to even read it! It remains the only prophecy that comes with a warning to those who refuse to "know and discern" its message. Yeshua alone fulfills this description—not to mention a plethora of other prophecies.

While Yeshua was rejected by the religious and political leaders of his day, there were many contemporary Jews that not only believed in Him, but were willing to be martyred rather than deny Him! This Man is the only one whose life has changed the way we date time, i.e., BC and AD.

Millions from around the world have received this message originally carried by a few Galilean Jews of no repute. People of faith from all eras have come to realize that salvation is a gift from God, not merited (Genesis 15:6; Isaiah 62:11 and 64:5–7; Acts 4:12; Romans 4). All of the Messianic prophecies found in the Tanakh have either been fulfilled in His first advent, or will be fulfilled at His return. It seems to me that either one can fear the "curse of the sages" upon those who contemplate this prophetic text, or "fear YHVH" and the curse upon those who reject His warning and command!

"I call heaven and earth to witness against you this day, that I have set before thee life and death, the blessing and the curse; therefore choose life, that thou mayest live, thou and thy seed; to love YHVH thy God, to hearken to His voice, and to cleave unto Him; for that is thy life, and the length of thy days; that thou mayest dwell in the land which YHVH swore unto thy fathers, to Abraham, to Isaac, and to Jacob, to give them."
Deuteronomy 30:19–20 JPS

8

THE DIVINE
TRIUNE NATURE OF GOD

As described earlier in the Seder tradition, the middle matzah is removed from its "presence" amidst the other two matzah; broken in two, wrapped and hidden away as in burial; found by those who seek; returned to the Seder leader who pays the redemption price (serving as priest); then a piece is given for each person to partake.

Believers in Messiah who understand Yeshua's place in the trinity vividly recognize its connection to the three matzot on the Seder plate: the middle Person of the Godhead left His place in Heaven; was cut off, wrapped in a burial cloth and hidden in a tomb for three days; returned to His heavenly abode, having paid the redemption price as our Messianic High Priest; and is found and shared by everyone who seeks. When Yeshua implemented this ritual at His last Seder, He was instituting the first element of Communion.

YHVH God, unique in His divine nature, is *echad*—a singular Divine Being manifest as three distinct entities. God calls married couples "echad:" clearly two distinct persons now meant to become one unity:

> *"Therefore shall a man leave his father and his mother, and shall cleave unto his wife, and they shall be one flesh."*
> **Genesis 2:24 JPS**

A plurality of gods would also be called *elohim,* but these deities all have distinctly different natures and desires. The three entities of the Godhead may have distinctive functions, but are of one will and nature. They uniquely share qualities of perfection such as: truth, goodness, eternality, omniscience, omnipotence, omnipresence, righteousness, faithfulness, and agape love. Scripture proclaims that the Creator is manifest through His handiwork:

> *"The heavens declare the glory of God, and the firmament showeth His handiwork; Day unto day uttereth speech, and night unto night revealeth knowledge;"* **Psalm 19:2–3 JPS**

The New Covenant insists that God's presence and self-revelation are so overarching that humanity has no defense for denying Him!

> *"For since the creation of the world His invisible attributes, His eternal power and divine nature, have been clearly seen, being understood through what has been made, so that they are without excuse."* **Romans 1:20 NASB**

YHVH also magnifies His Triune nature in what was seen from the beginning: time (consisting of past, present, and future), matter and space (consisting of height, width, and depth) and earth (consisting of land, water, and sky):

"And God said: 'Let the waters under the heaven be gathered together unto one place, and let the dry land appear.' And it was so. And God called the dry land Earth, and the gathering together of the waters called He Seas; and God saw that it was good." **Genesis 1:9-10 JPS**

All members of the Godhead participated in the Creation: YHVH the Father spoke the world into being, the Spirit prevailed over the waters of the Earth, and Yeshua was the Word of God that would manifest as the Light which was Good. (Celestial lights that supported life on Earth were not positioned until day four of Creation.)

"In the beginning God created the heaven and the earth. Now the earth was unformed and void, and darkness was upon the face of the deep; and the spirit of God hovered over the face of the waters. And God said: 'Let there be light.' And there was light. And God saw the light, that it was good; and God divided the light from the darkness." **Genesis 1:1–4 JPS**

Yeshua clearly identifies Himself as the Light that was in the world. John's gospel also identifies Yeshua as both the Light and the Word:

"In the beginning was the Word, and the Word was with God, and the Word was God. He was in the beginning with God. All things came into being through Him, and apart from Him nothing came into being that has come into being. In Him was life, and the life was the Light of men. The Light shines in the darkness, and the darkness did not comprehend it."
John 1:1-5 NASB

The prophet Isaiah supports this phenomena when he spoke of a faithful servant of YHVH who would be given a body in the womb to bring salvation to Israel and the nations:

"And now saith YHVH that formed me from the womb to be His servant, to bring Jacob back to Him, and that Israel be gathered unto Him—for I am honourable in the eyes of YHVH, and my God is become my strength—Yea, He saith: *'It is too light a thing that thou shouldest be My servant to raise up the tribes of Jacob, and to restore the offspring of Israel; I will also give thee for a light of the nations, that My salvation may be unto the end of the earth.'"* **Isaiah 49:5–6 JPS**

From a Messianic perspective, we see the second Person of the Godhead charged with a task that requires a human body and being brought into the world. This Servant of God is not only sent to restore Israel's relationship with the heavenly Father, but to be a spiritual light bringing salvation to all nations.

"Violence shall no more be heard in thy land, desolation nor destruction within thy borders; but thou shalt call thy walls Salvation, and thy gates Praise. The sun shall be no more thy light by day, neither for brightness shall the moon give light unto thee; but YHVH shall be unto thee an everlasting light, and thy God thy glory." **Isaiah 60:18–19 JPS**

This is a futuristic prophecy of the restoration of Jerusalem, when it becomes a place of worship for all peoples. It does not say the moon and stars will no longer shine on Earth, but it does seem to imply that in Jerusalem, where Messiah establishes His throne, that YHVH God will be the Sustaining Light! This Light first presented in Genesis 1 can very well be discerned as the Second Member of the Godhead.

9

MESSIAH'S DEATH AND RESURRECTION IN PROPHECY

The Tanakh includes numerous verses which have prophetic snippets that point to the death of God's Servant, Israel's Messiah. Isaiah 41–53, known as "the Servant" passages, paint a contrasting picture of God's servant Israel the nation and God's Servant Israel the Messiah (to distinguish between the two, only Servant Messiah will be capitalized). From the first reference to this Servant Messiah in Isaiah 42, we learn that He will "fail and be crushed," while the final chapter, Isaiah 53, gives complete details. Part 1 of this chapter will discuss what Isaiah says about the purpose of Messiah's death. Part 2 will look at Psalm 22, the most prophetically encapsulated portion of Scripture which foreshadowed how the Messiah would be put to death. Part 3 will look at the significance of His resurrection in fulfillment of the Feast of Firstfruits, as well as a frequently overlooked passage that provides insight into the timing of His death.

1. The Purpose of Messiah's Death

These Servant passages in Isaiah 41 to 53 contrast the unfaithful servant of God first introduced in Isaiah 41 as national Israel, with God's faithful Servant Messiah, as depicted in Isaiah 42-53. While the comparison between the two is striking and worth studying, this section will focus on what they tell us is the purpose for which Messiah had to die. Besides being told what His fate will be, we are also informed that His death will not occur until after He accomplishes the purpose for which He was sent by YHVH God. He may seem to fail in the eyes of national Israel and the nations, because the Messianic Kingdom will not be established at the time of His First Advent. However, in the eyes of God and the underlying spiritual purposes of His Coming, He will succeed! God will allow, even orchestrate, that His righteous Servant be put to death, enabling His unfaithful servant, along with any who repent, to live:

> "Behold **My servant,** whom I uphold; *Mine elect, in whom My soul delighteth; I have put **My spirit upon him**, he shall make the right to go forth to the nations. He shall not cry, nor lift up, nor cause his voice to be heard in the street. A bruised reed shall he not break, and the dimly burning wick shall he not quench; he shall make the right to go forth according to the truth.* **He shall not fail nor be crushed, till he have set the right in the earth; and the isles shall wait for his teaching.** *"* **Isaiah 42:1–4 JPS** (emphasis added)

These opening verses about this Servant reveal that He walks in the ways of YHVH revealing God's true nature and heart, while Israel's spiritual leaders had misrepresented and misled the people. They were meant to be representatives of God to the nations, but the peoples of the world remained in darkness, bound by sin and without hope, light and truth! Levitical priests expected the people to come to the Temple and bring their sacrifices with them. They deemed those who did not come with offerings, and those living immoral or worldly lives, as having condemned themselves and having no hope.

In contrast, this Servant of God would establish the true essence of the Torah and YHVH's righteousness, going out to share God's Word in a spirit of humility and compassion. He served the needs of all who hungered for blessings and hope: Jews, Gentiles, rulers, slaves, adults, children, God-fearing and sinners… In death, He provided Himself as the atoning sacrifice required to fulfill the Torah and free from condemnation all who would put their trust in Him:

> *"Behold, My servant shall prosper, he shall be exalted and lifted up, and shall be very high. According as many were appalled at thee—so marred was his visage unlike that of a man, and his form unlike that of the sons of men—So shall he startle many nations, kings shall shut their mouths because of him; for that which had not been told them shall they see, and that which they had not heard shall they perceive."* **Isaiah 52:13–15 JPS**

The verses above give a synopsis of the purposes accomplished through His death. He would prosper (שכל), or

more literally "act prudently." He would return to His rightful
position of glory in the high Heavens. "His-Story" would
not die with His mortal body, but be told from Jerusalem "to
the ends of the Earth." Despite the horrific outcome of this
Servant's life, many would want to follow Him. As spoken of in
the Torah (Deuteronomy 4:29), and the Sermon on the Mount
(Matthew 7:7), YHVH God would give spiritual illumination
to all who sincerely seek Him. He also speaks of a time when
all Israel will repent and accept their Messianic King at His
Second Advent:

> *"And so all Israel will be saved; just as it is written, "THE
> DELIVERER WILL COME FROM ZION, HE WILL
> REMOVE UNGODLINESS FROM JACOB. THIS IS
> MY COVENANT WITH THEM, WHEN I TAKE AWAY
> THEIR SINS."*[12] **Romans 11:26-27 NASB**

Messiah will return to Earth to deliver Israel from a time of
great travail (Jeremiah 30:7), establish His Messianic Kingdom
over all nations (Psalms 2 and 110; Daniel 7:13-14), reverse the
curse of death (Genesis 2:16–17), give eternal life (Ezekiel 37; 1
Corinthians 15), and a shared inheritance to all who have called
upon His name (Psalm, 16; Jeremiah 12:14-17; Hebrews 11).
He will fulfill every promise He has made to the world when He
restores the glory of His original creation (Isaiah 11):

---

12   Romans is referring back to prophecies from Isaiah 27:9, 59:20-21, and
     Psalms 14:7, 53:6.

"I will put animosity between you and the woman, and between your descendant and her descendant; he will bruise your head, and you will bruise his heel." **Genesis 3:15 CJB**

"But with righteousness shall he judge the poor, and decide with equity for the meek of the land; and he shall smite the land with the rod of his mouth, and with the breath of his lips shall he slay the wicked. And righteousness shall be the girdle of his loins, and faithfulness the girdle of his reins. And the wolf shall dwell with the lamb, and the leopard shall lie down with the kid; and the calf and the young lion and the fatling together; and a little child shall lead them."
Isaiah 11:4-6 JPS

2. The Manner of Messiah's Death

No portion of Scripture more accurately describes the crucifixion than Psalm 22. It precedes the most renown psalm (Psalm 23), yet few are familiar with it. David recorded it as if he was living through this scenario, yet certain portions bear no resemblance to his own life. It vividly describes the effects of crucifixion upon its victims, despite the fact this form of torture had not yet been conceived. Crucifixion[13] is thought to have originated with the Persians (fifth to sixth centuries BC), brought into the Mediterranean region by Alexander the Great (fourth century BC), and introduced to the Romans by the Phoenicians (third century BC), long after David's lifetime (tenth to eleventh

---

13   Reference sources concerning historical and physical effects of crucifixion include: NCBI: U.S. National Library of Medicine National Institutes of Health; Encyclopedia Britannica; learnreligions.com, Mary Fairchild.

centuries BC). David was thus given a supernatural prophetic experience of what his promised Seed would endure.

David and his Messianic Son did have some common experiences. Both:

1. were despised and rejected by many of their own people without reason

2. were perceived as threats to Israel's ruling kings (David by Saul; Yeshua by Herod)

3. did not lift a hand in defense against those in authority over them

4. faithfully and sacrificially forgave those among their kin who wronged them

5. were mocked by those who believed God would not rescue them

6. resolutely trusted and praised God when faced with great trials

7. were anointed as God's chosen kings before the nation would know or receive them (David by Samuel).

The portions of Psalm 22 noted below are situations David never personally faced, yet his Messianic son did:

"My God, my God, why hast Thou forsaken me, and art far from my help at the words of my cry?" **Psalm 22:2 JPS**

This exact quotation is declared by Yeshua on the cross (Matthew 27:46). Whenever David expressed the inability to feel God's presence, it was due to his own sins. In the psalms where David endures pain without cause, it is God's presence that strengthens him. However, Psalm 22 is regarding a time when God's servant is suffering without cause, and God's presence is still far off, adding to the agony:

> *"Be not far from me; for trouble is near; for there is none to help. Many bulls have encompassed me; strong bulls of Bashan have beset me round. They open wide their mouth against me, as a ravening and a roaring lion."* **Psalm 22:12–14 JPS**

The psalmist describes himself surrounded by enemies and crying out to God for help. The oppressors are compared to the strong bulls of Bashan (Ezekiel 39:18), mighty and formidable if aroused against someone. In his vision, these bulls have cut off any chance of escape. David also compared these enemies to ravenous and roaring lions that would intimidate and brutally devour their prey. In the context of Messiah's sufferings, the text is envisioning the hostile Roman soldiers surrounding Him, and a mocking multitude being entertained by the macabre.

Victims of crucifixion were first subjected to relentless scourging and brutal maiming. They were then forced to drag the crossbeam on which they would be hung to the execution site. They would have been stripped of all clothing to further humiliate them. The crossbeam would be attached, and the person hoisted up onto the upright stake already secured in the ground. Their hands would be secured to the crossbeam at the wrists and their feet to the stake at their ankles, by either ropes or nails as in Messiah's case. Above their head would be a sign stating their name and crime. Messiah's read: "This is Yeshua King of the Jews" (Matthew 27:37).

Death by crucifixion was a cumulative result of massive suffering. The scourging and maiming preceding it would have already weakened them and disfigured their appearance. Blood and bodily fluids would pour out and cause severe hemorrhaging and dehydration. The shock from such excruciating pain would sometimes mercifully lead to unconsciousness and death. The bones of the victims became disjointed, so they could not lift themselves up and breathe, resulting in asphyxiation. Often a person would go into cardiac arrest, their hearts figuratively "melting like wax." Even their mouths would be so dry that trying to move one's tongue to speak or swallow would seem impossible, perhaps describing the effort it might have taken the Messiah to declare, "It is finished," before giving up His Spirit (John 19:30).

The Roman guards would not be allowed to leave the scene to go home until all victims were dead. To expedite their demise, the Romans would usually break a shinbone so the victim could not lift their bodies up for air. In Yeshua's case, He expired before "any bones were broken," a prophetic requirement of the Passover sacrifices. These physical experiences common in crucifixion were vividly and accurately described by David centuries earlier:

> "I am poured out like water, and all my bones are out of joint;
> my heart is become like wax; it is melted in mine inmost parts.

My strength is dried up like a potsherd; and my tongue cleaveth to my throat; and Thou layest me in the dust of death. For dogs have encompassed me; a company of evil-doers have inclosed me; like a lion, they are at my hands and my feet. I may count all my bones; they look and gloat over me. They part my garments among them, and for my vesture do they cast lots." **Psalm 22:15–19 JPS**

The use of "dogs" refers to the scavenger-like behavior of wild dogs as they would brutally gnaw at a carcass. "Dogs" also can refer to false teachers, which is a fitting description of those who would reject the prophetic Word of God "in the flesh:"

"And the Word became flesh, and dwelt among us, and we saw His glory, glory as of the only begotten from the Father, full of grace and truth." **John 1:14 NASB**

Crucifixion and nakedness would make a victim's protruding bones easy to count. The guards cast lots for his clothes, completely indifferent to His sufferings, while the crowd continued to enjoy the spectacle of bloody torture on display before them. One portion of this passage needs to be looked at more closely, because the Jewish and most Christian translations clearly differ:

"… a company of evil-doers have enclosed me; like a lion, they are at my hands and my feet." **Psalm 22:17b JPS**

"… A band of evildoers have encompassed me; They pierced my hands and my feet." **Psalm 22:16b NASB**

The two words in question here are lion and pierced. In the JPS version (as well as Complete Jewish Bible and NET Bible), the Hebrew word אֲרִי, is accurately translated as "lion." Most Christian Bibles translate it as "pierced." The Hebrew word חלל, found in Isaiah 53:5, meaning "pierced" or "wounded," is not found in Psalm 22. The word for "lion" is found three times in this Psalm: 22: verses 13, 16 and 21 (13,17 and 22 in JPS). This same word is translated "lion" in 22:13 and 21, and likewise it should be translated "lion" in verse 16. The meaning contextually stays the same: evildoers surrounded the dying Savior like lions encircle their prey, and their claws and teeth would wound and pierce the bodies of their victims.

Another verse in the Torah foreshadows how the Messiah would die and why. It was written by Moses and describes anyone who "hangs on a tree" as being one disapproved of or cursed by God:

> *"And if a man have committed a sin worthy of death, and he be put to death, and thou hang him on a tree; his body shall not remain all night upon the tree, but thou shalt surely bury him the same day; for he that is hanged is a reproach unto God; that thou defile not thy land which YHVH thy God giveth thee for an inheritance."* **Deuteronomy 21:22–23 JPS**

YHVH the Father had to forsake the Son while He was dying, for He was made a curse for us. Yeshua is the Shepherd of Psalm 23 who "restores our souls;" we are the sheep:

"WHO COMMITTED NO SIN, NOR WAS ANY DECEIT FOUND IN HIS MOUTH; and while being reviled, He did not revile in return; while suffering, He uttered no threats, but kept entrusting Himself to Him who judges righteously; and He Himself bore our sins in His body on the cross, so that we might die to sin and live to righteousness; for by His wounds you were healed. For you were continually straying like sheep, but now you have returned to the Shepherd and Guardian of your souls." **1 Peter 2:22–25 NASB**

3. The Timing of Messiah's Resurrection

It has already been established that Yeshua fulfilled the Spring Appointments (page 88), which would have required Him to be resurrected on the Feast of Firstfruits. To understand the significance of His Resurrection on the Day of Firstfruits, we need to look once more at what Leviticus says about this Appointed Time with God:

"And YHVH spoke unto Moses saying: 'Speak unto the children of Israel, and say unto them: **When ye are come into the land which I give unto you,** *and shall reap the harvest thereof, then ye shall bring the sheaf of the first-fruits of your harvest unto the priest. And he shall* **wave the sheaf before YHVH, to be accepted for you; on the morrow after the sabbath the priest shall wave it**... *And ye shall eat neither bread, nor parched corn, nor fresh ears, until this selfsame day, until ye have brought the offering of your God; it is a statute for ever throughout your generations in all your dwellings.'"* **Leviticus 23:9-11, 14 JPS** (emphasis added)

What needs to be emphasized is that this Spring Appointment, unlike the other two, was not to be initiated **Until** they were in the land of Canaan. The sheaf of this new grain would be gathered together from the people. Then the High Priest would meet with God that morning following the weekly Sabbath, and wave it before YHVH as an unleavened offering on behalf of His people. Therefore, the first occasion they would have had to provide this offering would have been through Eleazar their High Priest (Deuteronomy 10:6), at the time when Joshua brought them into the Promised Land:

"And the children of Israel encamped in Gilgal; and they kept ***the passover*** *on the fourteenth day of the month at evening in the plains of Jericho. And they did* ***eat of the produce of the land on the morrow after the passover*** *[Feast of Unleavened Bread],* ***unleavened cakes*** *and parched corn, in the selfsame day.* ***The manna ceased on the morrow,*** *after they had eaten of the produce of the land; neither had the children of Israel manna any more; but they did eat of the fruit of the land of Canaan that year."* **Joshua 5:10-12 JPS** (emphasis added)

What should be noted is that after forty years of God's Divine provision of manna, that the first Day of Unleavened Bread would be the last day they would ever see it. In that same season, on the morning following that Sabbath, Eleazar the High Priest would have stood alone before YHVH waving an unleavened sheaf from the first crop in Canaan, to be accepted on behalf of this new and holy nation! How fitting that at the very season when the manna from Heaven would no longer be given, Messiah was raised up from the ground as an acceptable unleavened offering on behalf of His people:

> *"So they said to Him, 'What then do You do for a sign, so that we may see, and believe You? What work do You perform? Our fathers ate the manna in the wilderness; as it is written, 'HE GAVE THEM BREAD OUT OF HEAVEN TO EAT.' Jesus then said to them, 'Truly, truly, I say to you, it is not Moses who has given you the bread out of heaven, but it is **My Father who gives you the true bread out of heaven. For the bread of God is that which comes down out of heaven, and gives life to the world'** ... 'Truly, truly, I say to you, he who believes has eternal life. **I am the bread of life**. Your fathers ate the manna in the wilderness, and they died. This is the bread which comes down out of heaven, so that one may eat of it and not die.'"* **John 6:30-33; 47-50 NASB** (emphasis added)

Scripture gives examples of miraculous resurrections shortly after death (1 Kings 17:17–24; Luke 8:49–57), and Lazarus after four days in the tomb (John 11); however, all who rose would eventually die again. Yeshua predicted His own resurrection would be on the third day. He was fulfilling another Messianic prophecy given by King David:

> *"Therefore my heart is glad, and my glory rejoiceth; my flesh also dwelleth in safety; For Thou wilt not abandon my soul to the nether-world; **neither wilt Thou suffer Thy godly one to see the pit.** Thou makest me to know the path of life; in Thy presence is fulness of joy, in Thy right hand bliss for evermore."* **Psalm 16:9–11 JPS** (emphasis added)

In this psalm, David testifies that He would die and decay, but God would someday raise him up. However, he prophesies of God's "holy one" who would suffer death, but be raised up prior to undergoing corruption. Science tells us that the human flesh does not begin to decay until after three days. David gives thanks to YHVH for guiding him in this life, and showing him the path to eternal life and everlasting joy in the presence of the Holy One!

10

IN THE ORDER OF MELCHIZEDEK

⌒◦∽◦⌒

Why should one care who Melchizedek is? He only enters the scene once in Scripture, though he is referred to several times. He is both "a King and Priest"; his name means "King of righteousness"; and his land is called "Salem" or "Shalom," which means "peace" (though the Hebrew meaning is broader to include "harmony, wholeness, and prosperity"). Melchizedek arrives to break bread with Abraham (Abram) and bestow a blessing upon him; Abram responds by giving Melchizedek a tithe.

King David will prophetically speak of his Lord also being his High Priest. The author of the book of Hebrews exhorts the Messianic believers (living at the time when the Temple still stood), that they are to honor "their High Priest and King" by accepting what He had already supplied for them as a sacrifice, and not be led astray by the Levitical priests of their day.

To clearly understand the significance of Melchizedek as an example of the promised Messiah, we will look into the various accounts in Scripture where Melchizedek is named.

1. Knowledge of Melchizedek from the encounter with Abraham

"And Melchizedek king of Salem brought forth bread and wine; and he was priest of God the Most High. And he blessed him, and said: *'Blessed be Abram of God Most High, Maker of heaven and earth; and blessed be God the Most High, who hath delivered thine enemies into thy hand.'* And he gave him a tenth of all." **Genesis 14:18–20 JPS**

Melchizedek arrived on the scene following the miraculous conquest organized by Abraham against an alliance of four kings who had defeated and captured the peoples and goods from nearby kingdoms. Among the peoples kidnapped were those of Sodom, where Abraham's nephew Lot and his family had been living. Abraham had not only safely brought back his relatives, but also the other peoples and possessions that were stolen. Abraham and his men, along with the returning peoples, as well as the rulers of those who had been rescued, all had met in an area called the "King's Valley." According to Ancient Near East protocol, it was customary for the kings to pay a handsome tribute to the victor, which would include any recovered possessions, as well as other incentives, in hopes that the victor would relinquish the citizens to their original rulers.

Seemingly out of nowhere, Melchizedek had shown up at the King's Valley as king and priest of the Most High God! Where Melchizedek had come from was neither questioned nor told, yet Abraham could spiritually discern that he was not like the kings of the surrounding regions. This servant of the Almighty God had come to publicly confer favor upon Abraham before all who were gathered. Melchizedek first brought out bread and wine in an act of fellowship with Abraham, then bestowed upon him the blessing YHVH God had privately given to him in Genesis 12:

> *"And I will make of thee a great nation, and I will bless thee, and make thy name great; and be thou a blessing. And I will bless them that bless thee, and him that curseth thee will I curse; and in thee shall all the families of the earth be blessed."*
> **Genesis 12:2–3 JPS**

Melchizedek had come to represent the heart of the God he served, the Creator of Heaven and Earth. YHVH God was not only concerned about Abraham and his family, but also those dwelling in spiritual darkness. While Abraham remained a mere sojourner in the Land of Promise, I believe Melchizedek had been sent to point the lost multitudes to the one among them who could lead them to a knowledge of the One True God! They were privy to witness the faithfulness of Abraham's God to him in battle, and Abraham's faith in God, trusting neither in kings nor riches - but only YHVH!

Abraham had refused any compensation from the kings as a reward, so they would not think that they had made him rich. However, he did make sure that the allies who accompanied him were recompensed fairly. Then, he gave a tenth of all the bounty to Melchizedek in recognition that the victory belonged to YHVH. This is the first incident in Scripture where an offering to God is given through a "mediator." It was also given volitionally, not under compulsion as Mosaic Law required.

Another fact worth noting is that this is the first biblical record of bread and wine as a sign of fellowship between Almighty God and man, as administered by YHVH's priestly mediator. It seems to be a prototype of the bread and wine blessed by the rabbis on Shabbat, before being shared with the congregation. It also is a prototype of the bread and wine administered by church leaders as the sacrament of Communion. I find it compelling: 1) that neither party felt the need to include a blood offering to assure God's approval, even though Abraham's former offerings had always been blood sacrifices; and 2) that blood offerings would become the quintessential element required in the sacrifices made by the Levitical priesthood under Mosaic Law.

2. Knowledge of Melchizedek from David's Psalm

Mosaic Law forbid Levites to be kings or Davidic kings to be priests, yet Melchizedek is mentioned by King David prophetically in Psalm 110. God had given David a vision of one higher-ranked than he, whom David acknowledged as his king and priest by likening him to this pre-Levitical line:

> "A psalm of David. YHVH saith unto my lord: *'Sit thou at My right hand, until I make thine enemies thy footstool.'*...
> YHVH hath sworn, and will not repent: *'Thou art a priest forever after the manner of Melchizedek.'* **Psalm 110:1, 4 JPS**

King David, having been a warrior who also won many battles by the hand of God, would certainly have been familiar with the battle won by the patriarch Abraham, and his visitor, Melchizedek. YHVH also revealed to David, that one day "his

Lord" would leave the heavenly realm to reign on Earth. At that time, the power of the unrighteous would be destroyed.

Another interesting fact revealed to David in his psalm was that Melchizedek is a priest forever. This means he is still serving as a priest to the Most High God in some manner of immortality today! Scripture gives multiple examples of cognizance beyond the grave (i.e. 1 Samuel 28:3–19; Luke 16:19–31), as well as the assurance of immortality to all who put their hope in Him:

> *"But that the dead are raised, even Moses showed, in the passage about the burning bush, where he calls the Lord THE GOD OF ABRAHAM, AND THE GOD OF ISAAC, AND THE GOD OF JACOB. Now He is not the God of the dead but of the living; for all live to Him."* **Luke 20:37–38 NASB**

3. Melchizedek as a Prototype of our High Priest and King

Much of Hebrews 5-7 explains in what ways the priestly order of Melchizedek was a prototype of Messiah. The role of priest was always chosen by God and not assumed by man. In the Levitical system, it was inherited by genealogy whether the person was worthy or not. Those ordained like Melchizedek, were chosen because of their righteousness:

> "So also Messiah did not glorify Himself so as to become a high priest, but He who said to Him, *"YOU ARE MY SON, TODAY I HAVE BEGOTTEN YOU;'* just as He says also in another passage, *'YOU ARE A PRIEST FOREVER ACCORDING TO THE ORDER OF MELCHIZEDEK.'"* **Hebrews 5:5-6 NASB**

Records were kept of the length of time Levitical priests served: from age thirty until death. There is no record of Melchizedek's genealogy, nor the age he began serving... and his ministry has no end:

> *"... without genealogy, having neither beginning of days nor end of life, but made like the Son of God, he remains a priest perpetually."* **Hebrews 7:3b NASB**

Only once a year on Yom Kippur (Day of Atonement), could the Levitical high priest enter the Holy of Holies in Jerusalem behind the veil, and make reparation for himself and all Israel (Leviticus 16). God promised a new and everlasting Covenant to Israel (Jeremiah 31:31–34; Ezekiel 37:26–28), under a new High Priest of whom Melchizedek was a prototype. He would enter the Holy of Holies in Heaven to make a "one-time offering" of His own blood to atone for all humanity's sins:

> *"This hope we have as an anchor of the soul, a hope both sure and steadfast and one which enters within the veil, where Yeshua has entered as a forerunner for us, having become a high priest forever according to the order of Melchizedek."* **Hebrews 6:19-20 NASB**

Levitical priests received a tithe (tenth) from all other Israelites. Abraham, the father of the Israelites, gave his tithe to Melchizedek as higher-ranking. Since Levi was "still in the loins of Abraham" when this tithe was given, in theory, Levi had also paid a tithe to Melchizedek, regarding him as of a higher order:

"And, so to speak, through Abraham even Levi, who received tithes, paid tithes, for he was still in the loins of his father when Melchizedek met him. Now if perfection was through the Levitical priesthood (for on the basis of it the people received the Law), what further need was there for another priest to arise according to the order of Melchizedek, and not be designated according to the order of Aaron?" **Hebrews 7:9–11 NASB**

God's Divine plan required a mediator between Him and sinful humanity. It did not change under the New Covenant, but rather returned to the order that preceded Mosaic Law in an effort to accomplish what the law could not do. Yeshua, our High Priest, offered the final sacrifice necessary to save the world and restore shalom. No Levitical high priest nor Davidic king was ever able to bring peace even for all Israel. Our High King and Priest will come again to establish His earthly Kingdom in the New Jerusalem, bringing peace on Earth to all who receive Him!

"And having been made perfect, he became to all those who obey him the source of eternal salvation, being designated by God as a high priest according to order of Melchizedek." **Hebrews 5: 9–10 NASB**

ABOUT THE AUTHOR

HEIDI EFROS-AFFRIME and her husband, Scott, attended Dallas Theological Seminary together, where Heidi received a four-year Master's Degree in Theology and graduated with high honors. They have two sons (both happily married), two grandchildren, and many pets. They have opened their home to numerous people (and animals) through the years and have remained family to many. They now live in New Jersey, where they have resurrected the Hope of Israel Messianic Congregation in Cherry Hill (which they co-founded in 1991). Heidi is also a cancer survivor and discovered her calling as a chaplain while undergoing treatment, became C.P.E. certified, and worked both in hospice care and hospitals. Along with people, all God's creation, and various creative interests, she enjoys reading and travel. Her passion is experiencing God in whatever she does.

To place an order for books or to contact the author, email Heidi Efros-Affrime at: <u>HopeofIsraelNJ@gmail.com</u>

Dear readers,

I felt compelled to say something from my heart. I always had an inner awareness that God was there, even though I experienced very little self-worth or happiness growing up; I did well at hiding my pain. My personal justification for being alive was to make others happy. Despite an awareness of God's existence, it never entered my mind to seek Him—I didn't even know what that meant! But getting pregnant a decade after I was informed I couldn't, brought me to my knees. I would daily pray for me to be able to carry this child and for the health of this baby, though I still didn't know what it meant to seek God.

It was during the first year of my son's life that I noticed a dramatic change in the lives of two very free-spirited people especially dear to me. Both had gone on a journey seeking God and challenged me to do the same. They both pointed me to the Scriptures: one to my Tanakh (Jewish Bible) and the other to her Christian version of the Bible, which I was not ready to receive. I wanted to find the God of my people, so I began my search at the beginning (Genesis).

I was amazed by God's unwavering love and mercy toward my people despite their waywardness! Yet, there were always those who were different, who had a personal relationship with God and sought to know Him and trusted Him. As God is my witness, I didn't go into my search looking for a Savior; the concept was foreign to me. But as He proclaimed to Moses and the people, *"But from there you will seek YHVH your God, and you will find Him if you search for Him with all your heart and all your soul" (Deuteronomy 4:29).* I asked Him to help me do that, and just like my ancestors who searched, I found a personal God who knew me fully, loved me unconditionally, and has filled my life with a purpose and joy I'd never known. I am dedicated to my life's work—to know God and make Him known! No matter where you may be in your understanding of God, I encourage you to ask Him to make Himself known to you—He will!

May God bless you with His shalom,

Heidi